chartered
management

instant mana
taking control of work and l

J0663746

emotional
INTELLIGENCE

JILL DANN

HODDER
EDUCATION
PART OF HACHETTE LIVRE UK

The publisher has used its best endeavours to ensure that the URLs for external websites referred to in this book are correct and active at the time of going to press. However, the publisher and the author have no responsibility for the websites and can make no guarantee that a site will remain live or that the content will remain relevant, decent or appropriate.

Orders: Please contact Bookpoint Ltd, 130 Milton Park, Abingdon, Oxon OX14 4SB. Telephone: (44) 01235 827720, Fax: (44) 01235 400454. Lines are open from 9.00 to 5.00, Monday to Saturday, with a 24-hour message answering service. You can also order through our website www.hoddereducation.co.uk.

British Library Cataloguing in Publication Data
A catalogue record for this title is available from the British Library.

ISBN: 978 0340 945 919

First published   2008
Impression number   10 9 8 7 6 5 4 3 2
Year   2012 2011 2010 2009 2008

Typeset by Transet Limited, Coventry, England.
Printed in Great Britain for Hodder Education, part of Hachette Livre UK, 338 Euston Road, London NW1 3BH by Cox & Wyman Ltd, Reading, Berkshire.

Hachette Livre UK's policy is to use papers that are natural, renewable and recyclable products and made from wood grown in sustainable forests. The logging and manufacturing processes are expected to conform to the environmental regulations of the country of origin.

The Chartered Management Institute

The Chartered Management Institute is the only chartered professional body that is dedicated to management and leadership. We are committed to raising the performance of business by championing management.

We represent 71,000 individual managers and have 450 corporate members. Within the Institute there are also a number of distinct specialisms, including the Institute of Business Consulting and Women in Management Network.

We exist to help managers tackle the management challenges they face on a daily basis by raising the standard of management in the UK. We are here to help individuals become better managers and companies develop better managers.

We do this through a wide range of products and services, from practical management checklists to tailored training and qualifications. We produce research on the latest 'hot' management issues, provide a vast array of useful information through our online management information centre, as well as offering consultancy services and career information.

You can access these resources 'off the shelf' or we can provide solutions just for you. Our range of products and services is designed to ensure companies and managers develop their potential and excel. Whether you are at the start of your career or a proven performer in the boardroom, we have something for you.

We engage policy makers and opinion formers and, as the leading authority on management, we are regularly consulted on a range of management issues. Through our in-depth research and regular policy surveys of members, we have a deep understanding of the latest management trends.

For more information visit our website **www.managers.org.uk** or call us on **01536 207307**.

Chartered Manager

Transform the way you work

The Chartered Management Institute's Chartered Manager award is the ultimate accolade for practising professional managers. Designed to transform the way you think about your work and how you add value to your organisation, it is based on demonstrating measurable impact.

This unique award proves your ability to make a real difference in the workplace.

Chartered Manager focuses on the six vital business skills of:

- Leading people
- Managing change
- Meeting customer needs
- Managing information and knowledge
- Managing activities and resources
- Managing yourself

Transform your organisation

There is a clear and well-established link between good management and improved organisational performance. Recognising this, the Chartered Manager scheme requires individuals to demonstrate how they are applying their leadership and change management skills to make significant impact within their organisation.

Transform your career

Whatever career stage a manager is at Chartered Manager will set them apart. Chartered Manager has proven to be a stimulus to career progression, either via recognition by their current employer or through the motivation to move on to more challenging roles with new employers.

But don't take just our word for it ...
Chartered Manager has transformed the careers and organisations of managers in all sectors.

- *'Being a Chartered Manager was one of the main contributing factors which led to my recent promotion.'*
  Lloyd Ross, Programme Delivery Manager, British Nuclear Fuels

- *'I am quite sure that a part of the reason for my success in achieving my appointment was due to my Chartered Manager award which provided excellent, independent evidence that I was a high quality manager.'*
  Donaree Marshall, Head of Programme Management Office, Water Service, Belfast

- *'The whole process has been very positive, giving me confidence in my strengths as a manager but also helping me to identify the areas of my skills that I want to develop. I am delighted and proud to have the accolade of Chartered Manager.'*
  Allen Hudson, School Support Services Manager, Dudley Metropolitan County Council

- *'As we are in a time of profound change, I believe that I have, as a result of my change management skills, been able to provide leadership to my staff. Indeed, I took over three teams and carefully built an integrated team, which is beginning to perform really well. I believe that the process I went through to gain Chartered Manager status assisted me in achieving this and consequently was of considerable benefit to my organisation.'*
  George Smart, SPO and D/Head of Resettlement, HM Prison Swaleside

To find out more or to request further information please visit our website **www.managers.org.uk/cmgr** or call us on **01536 207429**.

Contents

CHAPTER 03

CHAPTER 04

CHAPTER 05

CHAPTER 06

CHAPTER 07

CHAPTER 08

Preface

Instant Manager: Emotional Intelligence is intended to give you ideas to tackle common issues faced by managers and leaders. The book is not an academic text or deeply technical overview. Rather, it is intended to be practical so it offers a number of case studies and useful explanations.

We are not all natural leaders of people; sometimes we become people managers reluctantly. A number of us come to be managers through promotion from technical roles (in my own case in Information Technology). Our backgrounds may have included a small amount of development on the people aspects of organising work with the majority of development usually related to technical know-how. Therefore, the advice and guidance in this book centres on ten questions about EI which most managers have to deal with on an everyday or occasional (but impactful) basis. The book is intended to get inside your world and to allow you to get inside the minds of other people across the globe facing similar challenges.

EI as a concept attracts controversy amongst management development providers, neuroscience researchers and practitioners from many disciplines. Some opinions rest on the premise that EI is the 'repackaging' of interpersonal and intrapersonal competencies – basically how you handle yourself and others. However, this does not acknowledge the research conducted into neuroscience in the last couple of decades. Most researchers accept that there are more forms of intelligence than the traditional sole measure of intellect; IQ. We would not like to be graded at work because of the size of our feet alone so why should we accept IQ as the only measure of adding value?

EI is an awareness-based intelligence. To be highly developed our EI requires us:

- to stop and think
- to control our impulses
- to use our innate intuition
- to be authentic with ourselves and others
- to manage our fears in leading others effectively.

It is no soft option since it deals with our hidden areas and gets to the root cause of any unproductive behaviour. However, it is very rewarding when relationships improve at work or in the home and success comes so much more easily.

It is not something that a manager can 'do unto others' without plunging headfirst into self-development themselves. It just does not work like that. However, some of the development can be very focused and aimed at specific objectives such as increasing revenue by increasing sales team optimism in adverse circumstances. Simple but effective management strategies can be put in place. Examples are given in each chapter without their turning into a workbook on the topic.

Universally each nation needs its talent pool to be as effective as possible in the face of increasing global competition. You may have recognised that many of society's ills stem from a lack of EI in the communities and workplaces. It is of note that welcome progress has been made in terms of introducing this topic into the curriculum for schools. A worthy ambition would be to introduce EI enrichment and education throughout school, college and university life. Students in first destinations with employers would be much more likely to stay and to be more successfully integrated in their new organisation using these competencies.

How to use this book

The chapters follow a logical sequence, however, for the butterfly reader each chapter is treated as complete in itself. Where associations are strong the reader may be referred to specific chapters elsewhere. I recommend you take a month or two to read the book, trying to devote a couple of hours a week to it.

1. As you read, take note of what thoughts, memories and feelings are provoked.
2. Go to any resources referred to in the text.
3. Debate topics with colleagues, seeking feedback and ideally teaming up with someone as a development buddy.
4. Follow the Instant Tips.

You will soon experience rewards from your developing understanding. When acting on the learning in the book, try to focus on the following:

- no longer acting in hindsight and having to clear up misunderstandings which duplicate conversations
- increasing trust in relationships and shortening the time taken to agree decisions and actions
- increasing energy and effectiveness under pressure, so that more gets done in less time.

Acknowledgements

There have been many people who have helped me with my EI books since I wrote the first one in 1999. I want to register how lucky I am to have them in my life and to thank them all enormously.

- Dr Cathie Palmer-Woodward who first introduced me to the topic whilst we worked on the launch of an Internet bank.

- Barbara Paterson has been a tremendous source of inspiration and experience as well as being knowledgeable on the validity and verification of assessments technically.
- Dr Ros McCarthy is a powerhouse and one of the best networkers I know. She has always been able to come up with a contact with the answer if I got stuck. She has also done 360-degree feedback on me aiding my own leadership development hugely.
- Keith Jones and Kim Shenton both edited and proof-read my first two books as well as contributing insights or examples and both have given me encouragement during the authorship of this one.
- Dr Sherria Hoskins and Dr Edel Ennis at the Department of Psychology, University of Portsmouth for their interest in EI case studies and evaluating the role of EI competence in post-graduates' first destination success.
- Sandie Pinches dealt with my extroversion by co-designing a process for drafting the chapters: 'What have they got to get, be or do?' She also has the most wonderful way with words and terminology to make the text accessible to a diverse audience.
- The key unsung hero of course is my husband, Derek, who has become a book-widower on four occasions now. He is a great sounding board for all my factual and fictional writing. His cooking has become even more superb during all those deserted weekends.
- But lastly and by no means least, Alison Frecknall, who helped me through a more testing authoring time than on the previous three occasions.

This book is dedicated to my Father-in-Law, Frank Dann, who sadly aged 96 left this world before his time in May 2007.

01

What is Emotional Intelligence (EI)?

Emotional Intelligence (EI), or a lack of it, is manifested in different situations in a variety of ways. You might have seen a person facing an awkward situation which they tackled well regarding how people felt and what occurred. People heard them playing back accurately perceptions about how they felt. You on the other hand, left the room feeling baffled unable to see the point and with no grip on the situation at all. You may have found that others discuss how a meeting went with a totally different slant on what occurred to your own recollection. You cannot fathom why people behaved the way they did and you feel that they did not understand you at all.

These examples highlight high and low Emotional Intelligence and the significance of the gap from one to the other. As a person who develops greater Emotional Intelligence, the process will demystify other people for you and you will understand 'difficult' people and the roots to their behaviour (or gain the skills to explore them).

Format of the chapters: get/be/do

Each of the following chapters will make points about the topic that you have to 'get' – to understand the topic, related issues and the utility of having a different view from your original one. Next you will be challenged to 'be' differently having understood the key messages on the topic. Your 'way of being with others' means adjusting your attitude, your style of delivery so that what it feels like to be around you is different from before. You may not have changed your opinion or it may have been moderated. Finally, you are given a set of suggested 'things to do' which will implement the topic beneficially for your team and others in your world.

Introduction

Emotional Intelligence (EI), often measured as an *Emotional Intelligence Quotient (EQ)*, describes an ability, capacity or skill to perceive, assess and manage the emotions of one's self, of others, and of groups. All models or frameworks for Emotional Intelligence tend to include the following competencies:

- **Interpersonal:** You may read books on quantum mechanics for pleasure, but this doesn't necessarily mean that you get on terribly well with other people. This requires interpersonal intelligence – the ability to build rapport, motivate, influence and generally hit it off with other human beings. Great leaders have this intelligence in abundance.
- **Intrapersonal:** Relating well to other people isn't the same as understanding your own emotional inner life. Intrapersonal intelligence is the ability to be self-aware.

What is the business case for EI?

The cost of low EI in a business can be measured in terms of:

- **Time wasted in unresolved conflict.** People lose focus when they are churning over something they are incomplete about. They are not doing what your business needs them to do or they are just going through the motions. A person with high EI has resolved his or her issues and is able to deliver high performance.
- **Locked away potential.** It is estimated that most people have 30 per cent more potential than they currently bring to work. It is locked away because you have not created an environment where employees are motivated to share that potential. If you want an 'innovative' company, that means creating initiative in people (innovation exists through initiatives of people). Initiatives and creativity may occur to people but can they be expressed without fear of ridicule and explored thoroughly (not just one-dimensionally, such as through an engineering perspective alone)? High EI delivers initiative, innovation and creativity.
- **Lost customers, lower market share and lower referral rates.** The business model developed for the first Internet bank in the UK introducing customer relationship management produced a number of thought-provoking statistics. It is 16 times harder to win back a dissatisfied customer than it is to find a new one. You may not have the market share that your product warrants due to the quality of service surrounding sale and maintenance of your product. To convert a satisfied customer to an advocate of your organisation requires excellent products and fantastic service. Advocacy will bring you five new customers at a very low cost of acquisition. High EI in

customer service leads to sustainable, profitable relationships with customers, in your supply chain and in team processes within the company.

● **Costs associated with stress-related illnesses.** There is a strong link between body and mind in terms of health. Low EI can be related to living a more stressed life than is beneficial for health. Group dynamics can be such that the combined EI of the group is lower than the individual's within it. Most businesses rely on good teamwork for effectiveness of operations. High EI brings enhanced teamwork and reduced stress.

What is the personal case for EI development?

Consider this. You are on holiday touring India. You've had a long and exhausting day visiting some stunning parts of the country. You arrive back to the campsite and having enjoyed an excellent meal, you retire early, leaving all of your fellow travellers to party around the roaring campfire. Suddenly you are wide-awake and sit bolt upright to be confronted with:

There's a tiger in my tent!

Yes, it's that close! You have an immediate and very strong emotional reaction which causes you to do one of three things (and maybe some others too!):

- you freeze
- you leap out of bed and run like the wind
- you throw a heavy metal object at the offending animal.

You have just experienced an 'amygdala hijack'. To appreciate this, and emotional intelligence fully, we must first understand brain architecture.

Brain architecture

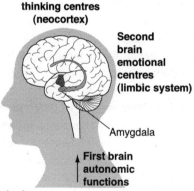

Figure 1.1: Key brain circuits

Understanding the structure and function of the brain is a starting point to learning emotional intelligence. A number of authorities on neuroscience have the following insights:

'The limbic system basically seems concerned with regulating our emotional states and drives, our motivations, our needs. Parts of it, for instance, make us look for food when we're hungry or look for water when we're thirsty or look for a mate when we want sex…. The power house of the limbic system is this little structure called the amygdala. The amygdala seems to be particularly involved in the extreme ends of the passions. Anger and violence and aggression on the one hand, but [also], as has recently been shown even in human beings – love and affection. These seem to engage the amygdala somehow in regulating and controlling the activities of the other parts of the brain, to direct the need into a constructive action.'

Colin Blakemore, Professor of Psychology,
University of Oxford

'Importantly, research reveals that the emotional brain (or limbic system) has the power to override the neo-cortex thinking brain. Consequently, for example, we can become (probably illogically or inappropriately) angry and lose control of ourselves.

…This primitive response very often gets us in trouble. It's an amygdala hijack. You have a sudden emotional reaction. It's very strong very intense and when the dust settles you realise it was very inappropriate: "Oh my! Why did I say that? Why did I do that?"

This is why our emotions are so much stronger in a moment of crisis or when we perceive a threat or when we're emotionally upset… why our emotions drive the neo-cortex, because that is the design that has helped us survive to this moment in history.'

Daniel Goleman

Using this insight to brain architecture, let's look at what happened when the tiger appeared in the tent:

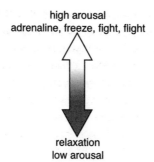

Figure 1.2: The physiology of performance – the body's short-term system

You may not have been confronted before by a tiger at close quarters, but you have had several close-call situations which have caused an adrenaline rush. You know the feeling: thumping heart, eyes wide open (to take in as much information as possible), churning stomach, your whole body focused on one thing, and a knee-jerk reaction – possibly flight.

At the moment of seeing the tiger, you moved from a state of low arousal (asleep) to one of very high arousal caused by the flood of adrenaline (or noradrenaline) released into your system.

Your reaction is based on experience of the same or similar situations. It is instantaneous and has no cognitive thought associated with it. It is a hijack because the part of your brain that is reacting works 80,000 times faster than the cognitive part of the brain so it is difficult to overcome the rapid adrenaline-based reaction.

Now let's take away the tiger and immerse ourselves in an everyday, normal situation. Are you reacting to someone at work in this way? The amygdala hijack is not saving your life in this case.

Figure 1.3: The physiology of performance – the body's long-term system

As we go through our days at work and play, we get emotional ups and downs. That's part of everyday life. If we are generally positive, the chemical DHEA (dehydroepiandrosterone) makes us feel good about ourselves and has positive effects on our physiology. If we are a negative soul, then cortisol cuts in to attempt to balance our well-being back towards a more negative outlook. The long-term effects of cortisol on our general health are known to be detrimental.

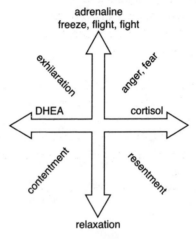

Figure 1.4: The physiology of performance – a lethal cocktail

And if there are frequent adrenaline surges as well, then our system becomes severely unbalanced and stress-related ill health results. This can manifest itself in heart disease and, it is believed, cancer. But consistently generally high levels of cortisol also have clear impact on our brain patterns, resulting in a lack of clarity. According to Chris Sawicki of Hunter Kane (HeartMath Europe), in a *business environment*, this means:

- projects that never take off
- projects that should never have been started
- cost overruns
- deadlines missed

- time spent in non-productive activity
- recalls on faulty products or services.

In terms of *personal impact*, it means:

- we are worried, anxious and confused about priorities
- we are time pressured, inefficient, and perform poorly
- we are tired, fatigued and frustrated
- we have a poor work/life balance
- we have elevated blood pressure
- we age more quickly.

The good news is that our brains were designed for clarity of thought, analysis, expression and creativity. To return to better health, we need to promote positive emotions and ensure that we spend our lives in the upper left quarter of the 'lethal cocktail' (see Figure 1.4), not in a state of permanent relaxation, resentment or anger/anxiety. How?

Our EI can take us there. Developing our EI can lead to greatly reduced stress.

What is self-awareness?

Consider what a life of being present in the 'here and now', experiencing distinct emotions and just *being*, might be like. The most outstanding results are achieved by *being* differently – much more so than by *doing* anything differently. This requires enhanced self-awareness.

What the sages said is true: 'The world is right here – all we have to do is to empty our minds and open ourselves to receive it.'

Consider, for a moment that your mind is preoccupied with the 'busyness' of your life – a lifetime of doing and achieving.

Do you live in the here and now? How self-aware are you?

The three levels of self-awareness

There are arguably three levels of self-awareness.

1. Awareness of the outside world – what you now see, hear, smell, taste and touch.
2. Awareness of the inside world – physical sensations such as neck ache, seating pressure points, the feel of your shoes and your skin in your clothes and emotions that come to you in your stream of consciousness.
3. Awareness of fantasy activity – all cerebral and limbic system activity beyond the present 'here and now'. Things that you feel, think and even emulate or simulate but are not actually part of the reality of the 'here and now'.

You may imagine yourself to be both strong and deeply in tune with your feelings, aware of others' emotions and adept at social intercourse to further your ambitions. Alternatively, you may feel that you are living a script and that you are not in control of the outcomes in your daily life.

If you have low self-awareness, the main learning outcome for you is to simplify your life by consistently recognising distinctions between reality (what actually happened or is happening) and fantasy (interpretation of what happened, your preferred outcome or projection of what may happen in the future). Most people 'daydream' about things they would like to happen or they recycle past events and create alternative outcomes. I have developed my self-awareness by using the fantasy element of our consciousness:

- to prepare for any meetings or interviews by creative visualisation or simulation of different outcomes
- to visualise or emulate how others may perceive me at the time, based on my answers to questions
- to predict how it may be in the first few days of a new piece of work.

Other levels of self-awareness have been about managing my responses, posture, tonality, stance, presentation (attitude) and so on.

Well-developed self-awareness takes you to another level of being and a richness of life. I expect it to be a lifelong journey and I forgive myself for reversing a step or two occasionally.

Reflector learning

Our Emotional Intelligence is both innate and shaped by circumstance and environment. The good news is that it can be enhanced in adulthood by increasing our ability to be proactive and reflective to accelerate learning.

A rational analysis of an emotive situation

Let me encourage you to be your own detective. Identify an incident where you felt that you were out of control, and do the detective work on it.

Imagine that a detective is interviewing you. Every time you start to wander away from describing what actually happened the detective would interrupt you and say, 'Just the facts, Sir, just the facts'. Now you have a factual description of what happened.

After you have described it to the detective, relate the whole thing as a child would tell a story. As children we embroider stories about occurrences especially after an emotional upset. The actual events become exaggerated or the wrong motives are assigned to the actions of others. If we allow this manufactured version of events to rule our recall of it, then we limit our possible futures. Taking an adult perspective is what the detective allows us to do based on the actual events and facts. If we contrast this with the made-up version, we see the differences that do us no favours in being successful in our future interactions. We have a chance to get it right next time and not repeat history. That is what this exercise helps us to do. Then consider the following questions:

- Highlight the difference between the facts and the story you fabricated or imagined.
- Look at what you made it mean, instead of another more fact-based interpretation.
- By creating a story from the facts of what actually happened, how has your story limited your dreams and aspirations?
- What has your story done to all your possible futures?

Looking at the facts, can you see alternative views of the reality – what actually happened? You do not have to limit your future by having a narrow view of your 'here and now'.

Persevere, as it is not unusual (if you are working on your own) to have to complete this several times before you can give up the meaning you have applied to the facts of the matter.

As a relatively new area of psychological research, the definition of EI is constantly changing. There are quite a number of different models and frameworks, but EI has its critics because of the lack of a single, scientifically-agreed boundary or even categorisation of the topic. Let's suspend disbelief for a few pages and explore the topic through story-telling.

Meet George and Michael, fictional characters we'll use to understand topics more thoroughly through story-telling.

George and Michael went to the same school and George was a couple of years ahead of Michael. They took similar academic subjects and both did well in qualifications. George became Head Boy and Michael noticed him, observing how socially at ease George was with people and how they referred to him often.

One day at work when Michael had joined the same firm as George, he spotted George in the gym and plucked up the courage to talk to him. George only remembered him vaguely but he was warm and engaging, putting Michael at his ease.

George: How are you settling in?

Michael: OK, but there are some tensions in the team which I haven't got an explanation for.

George: Did you know that both Susie and Leisha were up for your role before they recruited you?

Michael: No, I didn't know that. You're in a different section, how did you find that out? That's usually confidential to HR, isn't it?

George: Yes, well people often come to me. I help them think things through and get a better perspective on emotionally charged situations. It was the same at school.

Michael: I wish that happened to me. So where did you learn to do this? What's different about you?

George: I had a good family life. We talked a lot together, over meals usually. We sorted things out without too much shouting. Plus my Mum had a friend who was very successful in business and she taught me a lot too about dealing with difficult people – mainly by not being difficult yourself!

Michael: What do you mean by that last comment?

George: In my experience people find that when they become more self-aware the reasons why situations prove difficult are not what they originally thought. When we look inside, it may be that our style of communicating is different to others'. We as managers may need to adapt our style of delivering a message and the way we ask questions. Our style may not suit everyone.

Michael: But if you're the boss shouldn't the staff work to your preferred style? It's them that should be the most flexible.

George: Management isn't like that any more. We cannot be self-limiting because we need to develop others and release their untapped potential. Did you know that most people only use 5 per cent of what we have in terms of brain capability?

Michael: No, I didn't. I am surprised it's that low.

George: Yes, well we know a lot more about our brains these days scientifically and that is useful, as we can learn to use 100 per cent of them not just 5 per cent. It is by using our brain's capabilities differently and more fully that we can become more successful at work and in our home life. I'm not kidding – it's because I use my brain more fully that I get through life more easily. As well as what recent brain science tells us, some of the good old-fashioned ideas make sound business sense too. You know, phrases like 'It's not what you know, it's who you know that counts' and 'Manners maketh Man'. Well, the ability to form strong relationships and engage quickly with people is a key skill in private and business life. If that does not come naturally, you can learn it by understanding your brain more fully and gaining more experience – just like developing different muscle groups in your body by getting a new gym routine.

Michael: Hang on, what's the brain got to do with it? It sounds fascinating. Is that why you are different? Tell me more.

George: Think about it – even if you have exercised regularly after you have completed some new exercises, your body may be uncomfortable using those muscles for some time. Well the brain has different centres like muscle groups which we can be unaware we are using. They can help us more than we are used to. If we tone up brain activity, 'new man' can deal with more complex issues in our everyday lives. We can be less stressed and more effective.

Michael: But what makes you, and others, different?

George: Well, we all have very different intellects, or IQs, but it is more likely that you have different levels of emotional competence to me. I've got some material on this which I'll let you have later. Just let me explain briefly what I mean by these terms. Basically, our score varies with the conceptual model used for measurement, rather like kilo and pound weights are different in the gym. Whilst they are both measurements of weight they are scaled differently. So we need to explore how good we are at using our thinking to manage our emotions and our emotions to guide our thinking. We can then learn to use more brain capacity to deal with life's challenges and become smarter and wiser. After all, organisations pay for specific behaviours at work – every employee needs to think about this. That's the deal – knowing what you need to do and how best to get it done. So feedback on observed behaviour is useful and objectivity is essential on achieved outcomes, whether you are the employer, an employee or the manager.

Michael: It's great that it can be learned, but what's the best way of finding out what you've got as a basis for development?

George: The best measurement involves feedback from peers, other colleagues, staff that report to you, your boss, your customers, family, friends, professional associations and others. Self-assessment is possible but prone to unreliability. You may think that you don't have these brain centres, or muscle groups, but you have. You just haven't exercised them enough to notice.

Michael: So how do I get into training then?

George: Well, just like drawing up a new gym routine, we need to set out some reasons why you would want to get 'emotionally fit'. If you do not have some outcomes that benefit you and motivate you, changes will not stick.

Michael: Let me think about that and meet you for lunch. Are you free tomorrow?

George: That's good for me.

Some of the reasons to change can be extreme, as is illustrated by the following story. George had gone to an EI Conference in The Netherlands attended by people from 37 countries worldwide. He met people from South Africa who had told him stories which were very moving. One man we will call Simon, had found murder very easy under apartheid but after the regime had collapsed his guilt weighed heavily on him. Simon attended an EI course where people shared their stories and experiences in order to master their feelings and reach out to others who had suffered in different ways.

Simon struggled listening to the others' tales of their brutal treatment at the hands of parties on both sides. He became very angry as emotional memories surfaced of the rage and self-justification he felt at the time for his acts. After several days, he spoke up under the expert hand of an EI practitioner. Simon told the others in his group of his experiences. He was amazed at the love and forgiveness borne of compassion that he received from the group. He had felt totally alone in the world for many years.

Simon picked himself up after the course and worked very hard to buy himself his first car. It was a sorry specimen, very battered and with poor security but it gave him such freedom; he loved it. However, it was stolen one night and he missed it so much for the sense of freedom it had given him. With the car his world had grown large and now he felt trapped. He began to feel the rage grow in him once again. With his increased self-awareness since the EI course, he felt fear of his potential actions alongside this growing rage. He contacted his EI practitioner and she listened to him, helping him to calm down. She taught him some physiological EI exercises which interrupted his rage and got his mind and body to work in harmony. She also got him to think more broadly about his situation and come up with strategies to help himself which going on the rampage would not achieve.

He asked for help in his township and was amazed that he got it. Some people knew who had taken his car and they drove him to likely places. He explained what the car had represented to him and they understood his needs. He was an island no more. He received empathy and compassion. He began to heal. Then he began to help others to heal too.

He got his car back but, more importantly, regained his self-respect. The value of the process was his recognition of self-awareness, self-management, social awareness and the ability to manage relationships proactively.

He undertook further training in psychological techniques to increase Emotional Intelligence by increasing his skill in managing his emotions. This involved understanding the underlying chains of emotional memories which led to poor outcomes for him. By recognising his patterns of emotions which acted as triggers, he freed himself from losing self-control.

He increased his emotional literacy. He was able to get underneath the blanket emotions of rage and anger, confusion and frustration to the feelings which gave him more meaningful information about his drives. Underneath the anger was fear, envy, humiliation and other negative emotions. By tuning into these secondary emotions, he understood how to change his thoughts about a situation and his behaviour.

He learned to display genuine appreciation of others, empathy and compassion. His intuition increased as he learned to listen more actively, quietening the inner demons buzzing in his head. He was able to intuit what others were experiencing and shared this with them when summarising and checking his understanding of what had been said.

At the conference George also heard more stories about situations in Cyprus where Greek and Turkish Cypriots bridged their differences at events which used EI as the basis for the sessions. This allowed them to become more self-aware and self-managed, and with growing social awareness they were able to build sustainable relationships in these divided communities. There is still much work to do.

George thought about these extreme situations and then he thought about how conflict could be resolved or, even better, prevented in his own life.

This is not a soft option. Others may view the emotional competencies as 'pink and fluffy' – 'soft' skills. However, it is these skills which managers find the most challenging to learn.

How your behaviour as a manager impacts on the climate at work negatively or positively needs to be understood. There needs to be self-awareness and agreement on the manner in which you impact the performance of others. This is best done through 360-degree feedback mechanisms.

Greater Emotional Intelligence is learned through greater self-awareness. The less self-aware you are, the more you benefit from feedback from others and self-observation. So what does 'good' look like in a manager? The emotionally intelligent manager:

- is self-aware, motivated and perceives others accurately and fairly
- manages emotions to create winning outcomes
- is 'emotionally literate', recognising underlying emotions which blanket other feelings, with the ability to identify, recognise and understand the complexity of different emotions
- prepares for interactions by looking at the people and emotional process as well as the task and end goals so that they can anticipate others' reactions and help to manage their mental and emotional expectations
- thinks positively and is authentic, clearing things up, and does not easily quit if a difficult conversation is required
- has increased flexibility and is capable of adapting, being able to let go of out-of-date visions and plans
- promotes and creates a life/work balance, has good social skills and develops a sense of community and contribution
- is resilient when the going gets tough, seeking solutions.
- makes a commitment to personal development without feeling you need to be fixed and leaves behind old thinking, embracing a positive attitude to yourself and what you are learning
- inspires others in a natural way.

One thing you have to accept is that it can be daunting to manage others, especially for the first time. We are not always the ones who choose to be made a manager of other people – it sometimes just comes with the territory. If you have enough insight into how others see you or why others behave as they do, life can be enjoyable. If you do not, then you may have consequences which take a lot of your time to clear up.

For the willing manager, high EI can lead to being a better and happier human being. We use the term 'emotional outcome' which is a left-brained way of describing a right-brain activity. You have to be willing to use that less used part of your brain and to have a mental focus on 'ways to be' as much as 'things to do'. So when you write a task list you then also think of the most effective way of being to achieve it too as a manager of others.

Traditional measures	EI measures
profit / turnover	degree of trust
profit / total assets	generative relationships for truly innovative environment
profit / employee	low staff turnover
sales / employee	high customer retention and yield
total assets / employee	level of customer satisfaction
ROCE (return on capital employed)	referrals and community advocacy
levels of remuneration	relationship bank account
investment trends	investing in people
'specials' e.g. sales/sq m	size of personal network

Table 1.1: Comparing traditional business measures with EI measures

Equally, you have to recognise and accept responsibility for the consequences of choosing not to change and to recognise the poor pay-off in remaining the same. (For example, awkward relationships at work, low collaboration between family members, lack of psychological intimacy between you and your partner due to each others' unmet emotional needs.)

So what are the practical considerations?

- You may have no development budget and only this book for guidance, so willingness to learn is important.
- Since developing your EI to higher levels is an awareness-based process of taking the initiative for your own learning, it is necessary to begin with self-observation. Any lack of self-awareness and the willingness to start it will have an impact on your ability to direct your own learning.
- Since self-assessment can be inaccurate on its own, it is necessary to seek feedback from people involved in your everyday life (family, friends and colleagues) to get a more rounded perspective. You must be honest and not drop into self-loathing through truthfulness.
- Low self-confidence may be your starting point and you must use the feedback recommended to build a set of evidence of how you are in the world and why it is a source of strength. Be clear with people that you lack self-confidence and that their support in your process is vital.
- You need to have courage, compassion and humility since you cannot develop without experimenting. This process may involve feeling anxious to begin with. It can also be enormous fun and you need a sense of humour. You must be willing to learn from it all. Hence, seeking help from a friend, colleague or mentor is recommended unless you are enormously self-contained. Most of us feel alone in life: take heart and find courage!

Understanding terminology

So, you will not so much have to 'do' differently as to 'be' differently. It is about your way of 'being' around others and with yourself. For example:

1. You will identify 'traps' and how to 'spring them' so you stop acting out of hindsight and regret regarding your low EI behaviour.
2. You will need to process emotional memories, and patterns of emotions, to identify the first moment they cropped up in your life. You will learn to identify what happened and what you made it mean. How often do we recognise that our unacceptable behaviour stems from childhood experiences which are now running our adult life?
3. You will learn to be more intuitive developing an 'emotional radar' about acceptability of behaviour as a direct result in that moment and how continuing to behave that way may never have been nor is any longer appropriate.
4. How appropriate is your behaviour? You will become more aware of your ability to manage potential conflict – actively listening, being more intuitive, compassionate, achieving rapport easily, being diplomatic and tactful, asking more questions than stating opinions.
5. You may experience dips in self-esteem but you could be wise in developing new habits which reinforce positive self-image.
6. You will need to set up some personal rewards for experimenting to raise your EI. These vary for everyone and may not necessarily cost money. It may be as simple as having a pint with your mates, reading a novel, taking a warm aromatic bath, catching a movie or playing with your children.

7. You will need to know how to be emotionally literate, identifying specific emotions and their intensity. You will need to recognise that primary emotions such as anger, frustration and jealousy mask deeper emotions which are more useful and linked to motivation.

The key point is to make sure that you are:

● using your strengths as broadly as possible (laterally, thinking outside the box)
● using your strengths as often as possible and appropriately, i.e. constructively and not to manipulate
● using your strengths on yourself to crack some of the habitual behaviours which act counterproductively for you and others
● taking time to understand the impact on issues in your life of emotional competencies which are below strength.
● respecting the feedback enough to be called into action and commit to personal change.

Reading this book can help you to understand what motivates you and what dissatisfies you. No one can make you motivated to change.

In more detail

● IQ ('Intelligence Quotient') is defined as 100 times the Mental Age (MA) divided by the Chronological Age (CA) – see the work of Alfred Binet (1857–1911), French psychologist and inventor of the first usable intelligence test which is the basis of today's IQ test. IQ is thought to be fixed by age 11.

- EI is the abbreviation of the term Emotional Intelligence which focuses on more brain centres and abilities than does IQ. This can be increased through learning and self-developing.
- The neocortex in the front of our brains is our 'thinking' brain and the limbic system in the centre of our brains is concerned with our emotional memories and processing.
- When thinking of developing our Emotional Intelligence we are committing to utilising the mind/body link (mental/physical) and there are different approaches available to us:

  1. social and emotional competence development
  2. physiological techniques which can be learned and used for business success
  3. psychological and neurological techniques which increase our skill in the use of emotional memories and behavioural choices.

As a manager you are in the business leadership field so an explicit link between why people do what they do and the business outcomes is worth exploring and identifying. In terms of understanding roots to behaviour in addition to EI feedback, it is useful to have taken a predisposition or personality test (things you prefer or ways you behave without thinking about it). It is always possible to identify the positive aspects of any predisposition in an organisational context. One such test examines what is known as the 'Big Five' in the school of personality research as traits of personality (predisposition to behave in particular ways):

1. extroversion v. introversion
2. agreeableness v. antagonism
3. conscientiousness v. undirectedness
4. neuroticism v. emotional stability
5. open to experience v. not open to experience

The outcome for an individual is an understanding of preferences in terms of their thought processes and predisposed behaviour. Critically, if the individual is able to highlight their preference to approach a situation in a particular way this is a useful basis for communication within groups and other individuals in many organisational scenarios. The individual has a choice however, and may be motivated to behave against preference through the degree of utility of doing so or through learned behaviour (e.g. an introverted programme manager who communicates broadly during the professional day and reads a book in his hotel during the evening).

Trust radius

Definition: The degree to which you automatically expect other people to be trustworthy, to treat you fairly, and to be inherently 'good'; trusting until you have reason not to. The ability to rely on yourself, trust others and trust first.

Do you have the capacity and the value to consistently trust and trust again?

- Who do you trust? How much do you trust them?
- How much do you share with colleagues?
- How much do you trust yourself not to care if they judge you?
- Do you trust first without people having to prove themselves?
- As a manager, do you walk the talk? Do your subordinates have a sense of fairness in boundaries, policies, etc.?
- How do you address problems with subordinates or peers? Implement the 'no back talk' rule – you must not say anything about another person that you have not said to them first.

● Albert Mehrabian's studies of listening reveal that 7 per cent of meaning is interpreted from words (cerebral cortex) and 93 per cent from voice tone and body language (limbic system). Remember that the 'emotional brain' or limbic system works 80,000 times faster than the conscious cerebral cortex. This gives us an 'instantaneous reading' on believability and trust. Unless a speaker is believable, authentic, congruent in voice, words and body language, the listener will make judgements about the speaker's trustworthiness. Think of leaders you respect … and those you don't.

Consider compiling some force field analysis about your unreliable behaviour.

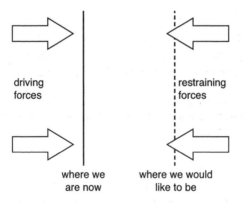

driving forces

restraining forces

where we are now

where we would like to be

Figure 1.5: Balancing forces for and against a proposition

Do you have self-respect issues and concerns about whether others respect you? Think back to when you were very young or explore this with a family member or friend.

● When was the first occasion you discovered that you were responsible for something?

- Perhaps a family member made you realise that you could be blamed for something. Maybe you told a lie to get out of being blamed.
- Try and think back to the earliest incident which generated in you a sense of being accountable for something.
- Why are you sometimes accountable and sometimes not?
- What actually occurred (the facts)?
- What did you make this mean about you?
- How could you view it differently?
- What does it mean about the way you behave now?

Summary

1. EI is an awareness-based capability. If you do nothing else, become more aware of the impact you have on others now that you are a manager.
2. Generate a greater understanding of how you learn optimally. There are considerable resources on learning styles that can be found through search engines on the Internet and in your local library. Peter Honey is well known in the UK for his original work in this area.

Explore the Emotional Intelligence of your team in the next week. When you next have a one-to-one with those staff that report to you ask them these questions:

1. What have you achieved since we last met?
2. Which of your qualities has helped your success?
3. To help you achieve everything you have planned, what do I need to provide, do or say?
4. Who has been the most helpful team member to you in achieving those things?

5. What qualities has that team member demonstrated and which felt the most supportive?
6. Of those qualities, which do you see as your strengths too? Can you capitalise on them more in the next month?
7. What can I do as your manager to help you demonstrate all of those qualities in the most helpful team member?
8. What can you do to incorporate those qualities into our current workload?
9. Who has asked you for the most help?

Word will get around very quickly that team collaboration is being monitored. Carefully noting and analysing the results will help you to model success in your team more closely.

- Research some good role models relevant to your field.
- Consider your own ability to be a role model – our capacity to influence and impact those around us is huge. Transformational team learning can emerge from understanding the roots of a role model's success.
- Collate the results in terms of qualities and share this at a team meeting to give each team member the collective ideas. Do not name who said what from the one-to-one meetings and focus on all the positives.

INSTANT TIP

Emotional Intelligence describes an ability, capacity or skill to perceive, to assess and to manage the emotions of oneself, of others and of groups.

How does EI affect me as a manager?

What do I need to understand about EI as a manager?

Improving self-knowledge and awareness of others' reactions is the foundation of most leadership and management development programmes. Managers and leaders must see themselves as others see them to be effective influencers to make work happen (the right work and right first time, on time).

Leaders need the most adaptive behaviour in order to respond to unplanned change and to be as visionary as possible for the organisation. One size does not fit all. Leadership is also about developing 'followship'; bringing on those who follow you. Leaders need to be highly self-aware, self-regulated, socially adept, strong influencers and good at relationship management.

They need a political radar, the ability to change cultures and the ability to network powerfully to strengthen the reputation and resources available to the business. How much of this is about industry or market knowledge, or innate intellectual intelligence? Certainly know-how and knowledge are important to success, but

Emotional Intelligence characteristics are picked out as identifiable in good role models 80 per cent of the time.

You might observe, 'If EI is so important, how come I know people who have been promoted but are really "hard"?' EI is not about being 'nice'. Some businesses are so much in crisis management that the rewarded leadership styles are coercive at worst or pacesetting at best. Raising EI collectively affects the climate of an organisation positively even if you are undertaking 'an impossible job in an impossible timescale'. When we deal with each other under pressure in a high EI way, there is an electrifying buzz.

The subject of management or leadership style has to be explored as many managers think one style will do for all people and situations. Modern management involves a range of styles, including coaching others to develop them so that they do better in their role. There are different emotional competencies needed at strength in carrying off different leadership styles.

What doesn't feel good to us normally doesn't feel good to others. But to understand the importance of this, we must first be in touch with our own feelings. Feelings are fundamental to our very thoughts and beliefs about ourselves. Denial of what we feel can invalidate us as a people. Unlike thoughts, feelings are non-negotiable and when we relate feelings of high self-esteem it is usually because we feel accepted.

Components of EI:
- **self-awareness** – knowing how you feel in 'real time'
- **emotional literacy** – being able to label emotions precisely and to talk about feelings with others
- **empathy and compassion** – the ability to feel and understand the emotions of others
- **balance** – being able to make decisions using a healthy balance of emotion and reason
- **responsibility** – taking primary responsibility for your own emotions and happiness; not saying that others 'made' you feel the way you feel.

How does EI affect me personally?

The key to answering this question is to be honest about why you have successful or unsuccessful relationships:

- Do you come away from meetings or one-to-one interactions with a different understanding from others?
- Do you experience confusion over upsets because you do not understand why it happened at home or at work?
- Is there a constant sparring with someone at work when it has nowhere to go in terms of benefiting either of you?
- Do you find that in ordinary life you are always finding fault with people serving you in a shop, restaurant or a hotel?

If you are a sales manager, the consequences of poor relationships are poor team performance, sales results and client base through dissatisfied customers or falling sales. If you are a production manager, there may be many missed opportunities to make the production process more efficient and effective because no one feels valued enough to tell you.

The point of being a manager is that you are put in a position to have an influence over others.

- Are you groping in the dark to be influential?
- Are you growing some molehill-sized struggles into mountains?
- How much time do you want to spend clearing things up?
- How productive are others around you if you have an outburst or, conversely, fail to communicate and hold everything inside?
- What is the impact on the value chain of the organisation if the incident gets transferred or recycled in other departments?
- What is your reputation?

● Do you have an overdraft in your relationship bank account?
● Is the person in charge of you the five-year-old inside who fails to own the consequences of their actions?

If you really own your own performance you have the opportunity to be an inspiring leader to others, conducive to achieving the highest performance.

Table 2.1 illustrates the role Emotional Intelligence has in routine management activities or functions. For each basic management function examples are given on how you can take into account the emotional and psychological aspects which are pervasive and continually improving.

Planning	Allocating resources	Organising	Monitoring	Control
Include ways staff can buy-in	Demonstrate respect, fairness and equity	Use a participative style but be prepared	Get staff to set measures and milestones	Be clear and robust – management, technical and quality
Reduce resistance and avoid sabotage	Consider stretch and diversity	Accept that change will happen and set expectations of staff	Negotiate to get a levelled workable plan as change happens	Risk management involves risk owners at the working level

Table 2.1: Management activities and functions relating to use of EI

The team can continually learn from recycling the learning, seeking more associations and applications of it.

You can bring many qualities that you have and allow others to experience them to heighten employee engagement at work. You recognise the balance between technical knowledge and how it flows and the social/emotional competencies which are all part of teamwork and collaboration. Each individual has to be accountable for their own EI (emotionally responsible) and what impact it has on the climate at work. Each individual must recognise when they get sucked into pack behaviour and when they hide how culpable they are for the treatment of others. EI is not a soft option – it is very challenging, a form of 'tough' love.

Thus, there are some things about being human which require us to see emotions as important and relevant to the workplace.

- We need to pay equal attention to emotional skills as to professional and technical skills – 50 per cent of time at work is wasted through lack of trust.
- We need to learn to recognise the triggers to behaviours which lead to bad results through familiar routes.
- Counterproductive behaviour has to be nipped in the bud so that better outcomes are achieved leading to repeatedly high performance and productivity.

It is vital that each individual builds their own business case for change whether it is physical, mental or tangible health and good relationships at work and at home. You must feel the impact of not changing and the broader consequences for yourself and your team if you continue as you are. The following sections outline what has to be considered in understanding Emotional Intelligence.

Supporting your CEO

Your Chief Executive may need your support as a manager with the many challenges posed by growth, such as resources being stretched too thinly. During periods of consolidation the challenge is to reduce operational inefficiencies to achieve maximum revenue. The economics of growth and EI are covered in more depth in the chapter on how customers benefit from EI (Chapter 6). Managers are involved in solutions to these challenges and there are factors to take into account:

- change readiness – the adaptability of staff and their willingness to respond flexibly to change positively
- goals and champions – someone senior has to agree priorities and the sense of urgency of goals, and get the commitment from team members to achieve them
- global businesses and markets have an impact and this creates the need for skills in working across multiple cultures, ethnicity and religious preferences
- leading across functions – departments need to work across the whole organisation without division and broken business processes
- legislative compliance – law is an increasingly complex factor for managers to navigate through, in both the domestic and international arenas
- flexibility in leadership during growth – consciously having more than one management style which flexes based on the situation and the climate at work, adapting to get better results; recognising that the softer competencies come into management style whether at the directive end of the spectrum or the supportive end:
  - **being** – self-awareness and self-regulation especially dealing with colleagues under pressure
  - **doing** – understanding impact of changes on yourself and being a role model for change: being 'fit for change'
  - **having** – getting a grip on one's own development needs, e.g. predicting skills, know-how and management development; creating 'headroom for growth' of individual leaders.

Emotional competencies within leadership styles

George, who we met in Chapter 1, relates the story of a CEO, a past boss, who demonstrated inflexibility in his leadership style and that led to situations which could not be handled that way. There are productive leadership styles which are appropriate at different stages of the organisation's lifecycle when going through change.

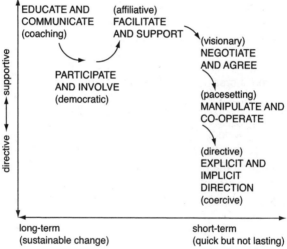

Figure 2.1: Dealing with resistance to planned change

George gave examples of the stages of the project and the styles that his boss demonstrated at each stage (see table overleaf).

George experienced considerable frustration at the complete mismatch of leadership styles. He did not get what he needed to support him.

If George had been an inexperienced manager then a *visionary* and *pacesetting* style by his boss in the early stages would have helped, provided that he was empowered to take the actions, under guidance. Then, with an agreed project plan, a

Stage	Leadership style
set-up and initiation stages	distant and hands-off
first stage of technical work	hands-on and directive or coercive with George's team members
second stage of technical work	critical and demanding detailed reports
build stage	unavailable and pulls resources to another project
test stages	involves users in work other than this project

mentoring/coaching style would have helped in directing the project and increasing the skills of his team as required. Where necessary in winning buy-in and support for the products and outcomes, an *affiliative* or *democratic* style would have been suitable at workshops and focus groups at design and build stages. His boss's attendance could have demonstrated his sponsorship of the purpose of the project.

What is evident is that clarity of communications is key through the reporting line where light is shed on the matters in hand and messages are not obscured in either direction. No one likes being treated like a mushroom.

Leading transitions

Michael relates to George his experience of misreading the signs in a team meeting. George deconstructs what happened, looks at alternative motivations of staff for their actions and discusses how meaning is applied to the behaviour of others.

Michael had to start-up a project to merge the IT department with that of a company being acquired. The new company had better technologies and reputation in the marketplace. An Information Systems (IS) Strategy Study needed to be set up to make best use of both companies' information assets and to meet the market and new opportunities from combined offerings.

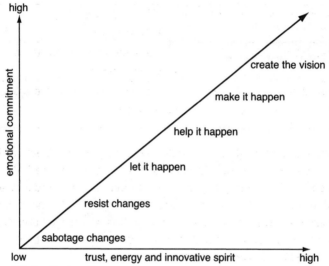

Figure 2.2: Leading transitions

- A number of staff were intensely excited about the possibilities in a newly merged IT department and company as a whole.
- A number were willing to help but were not quite sure how.
- Others were apathetic and some were angry and resentful to different levels of intensity.

Michael had to lead on a limited IS Strategy Study budget and he had an even more limited training and development budget for the integration programme. Where would you spend this money? Would you spend it at the bottom of the curve where emotional commitment and trust, energy and innovative spirit were low or lacking?

Michael had got everyone together to present a *fait accompli* of the Project Brief for the IS Strategy Study based on a mandate from corporate and programme management. After a period of silence when everyone took this on board, people began to object quite vehemently or enthuse about the opportunities. The emotional climate in the room was electric from quite different perspectives. Michael lost control of the meeting and was now feeling bruised having called it to an early close. He had told people he would rearrange things.

George got him to think about the staff being spread across the scale of commitment to change from active sabotage to making it happen and creating the vision. He encouraged him to meet the most passionate individually, whether they were potential assets or saboteurs. Where possible he could have small groups and create a participative atmosphere where they could feel involved. Chapter 7 explores how EI can accelerate management of change in more detail.

Before incidents like this occur, and time is lost clearing up and getting back on course, it is valuable to take a fresh perspective on emotions in the workplace.

The importance of emotions

Before the benefits of high EQ can be grasped, the bedrock of EI is acknowledgement of the importance of emotions in business as well as personal life. Consider this and record your thoughts and feelings. You may like to share your reflections and debate them with a friend or colleague.

Our bodies communicate with us through instinct, intuition and responses to stressors in our lives. This information is of equal importance to our thought processes. How many times have you gone against a gut feeling to discover it has turned out to be true and you could not find a rational reason why? Our bodies communicate with us and others to tell us what we need. It is essential that we accept the importance of our emotions for several reasons:

- The better our communication, the better we feel.
- Emotions help us establish our boundaries.
- Emotions have the potential to unite and connect us.
- Emotions can serve as our inner moral and ethical compass.
- Emotions are essential for good decision making.

Respect

All humans need to feel respected, even the least powerful. To show respect to someone we must respect their feelings. Respecting feelings includes asking about feelings, validation and empathy. Respecting someone means asking how they would feel before making decisions which affect them.

Validation

- Acknowledge, accept, understand and nurture feelings.
- To validate someone is to accept their individuality.
- Validation is one of the keys to Emotional Intelligence.
- Validating someone allows them to accept themselves.
- Self-acceptance is a key to high self-esteem.
- Often, the only thing we need is validation to feel better.

Think of a time when you worked really well not only in your job but also with the people around you. Ask yourself the following questions:

1. What was happening?
2. Who was doing what?
3. How did you feel about yourself and those around you?

Invalidation

Invalidation is to reject, ignore, mock, tease, judge or diminish someone's feelings. Invalidation goes beyond mere rejection by implying not only that our feelings are disapproved of, but that we are fundamentally abnormal.

There are many ways in which we are made to feel 'invalidated'. These might include:

- We are told we shouldn't feel the way we feel.
- We are dictated to not to feel the way we feel.
- We are told we are too sensitive, too 'dramatic'.
- We are ignored.
- We are judged.
- We are led to believe there is something wrong with us for feeling how we feel.

Psychological invalidation is one of the most counterproductive ways to try to manage emotions. It kills confidence, creativity and individuality.

Telling a person she should not feel the way she does is akin to telling water it should not be wet, telling grass it shouldn't be green, or the rocks that they shouldn't be hard. Each person's feelings are real. Whether we like or understand someone's feelings, they are still real. To reject feelings is to reject reality; it is to fight nature and may be called a crime against nature, 'psychological murder', or 'soul murder'. Considering that trying to fight feelings, rather than accept them, is trying to fight all of nature, you can see why it is so frustrating, draining and futile.

Communicating negative feelings

- Express your specific feeling (such as, 'I am afraid that ...').
- Ask for help ('Can you help me understand ...?').

- Avoid 'you messages' which put others on the defence.
- Avoid judging, labelling and criticising.

Effects of positive feelings

When our emotional needs are satisfied we feel better, and when we feel better we are more:

productive	creative	understanding
motivated	cooperative	empathetic
adventurous	open-minded	compassionate
patient	flexible	accepting
complimentary		

More desirable feelings which management can help create

respected	trusted	irreplaceable
acknowledged	appreciated	useful
supported	important	needed
helped	special	valued and valuable

Primary and secondary emotions

Primary emotions identify our unmet emotional needs (UENs); secondary emotions are not so clear. For example, if I say 'I feel ignored, I need to feel acknowledged', I am expressing a need to feel acknowledged. But if I say 'I feel angry', it is not clear what emotional specific need is unmet. Thus anger and frustration are blanket emotions which are secondary to an underlying primary emotion which if we identify it specifically gives us much more insight to what is going on. The ability to identify primary from secondary emotions is known as emotional literacy.

Emotional literacy

This skill is about the ability to speak about emotions in three-word sentences beginning with 'I feel ...', preferably stated using a primary emotion to provide more insight. This is similar to the concept of a coach directing a coachee to use 'I messages' which avoid using third-party phrases that disassociate the person from the message: 'I did this', not 'this happened'.

Examples of emotional literacy	Examples of what is *not* emotional literacy

I feel ...
    criticised
    unimportant
    disrespected
    bored
	I feel like ...
	I feel that ...
	I feel like you ... (this is a 'you' message in disguise)

In brain architecture terms, emotional literacy allows the brain to recall past events when similar situations and patterns occurred. These are located in the limbic system (see Chapter 1). This allows individuals to recall why they carry out this behaviour and what originally stimulated it or motivated them to feel a particular way. It is a clear capability necessary for self-awareness leading to self-management. It is also a prerequisite in effective communication with other people to express yourself accurately and share feelings.

What is the impact of my EI on the workplace?

Having understood what has to be considered regarding Emotional Intelligence as a manager of people, what is the impact of a manager's EI on the workplace? The majority of problems at work are from unmet emotional needs. The emotionally intelligent manager, then, knows how to identify and manage unmet emotional needs of both the customer and the employee. Conversely, a manager operating with low EQ is likely to engender negative feelings amongst employees.

Common negative feelings amongst employees

disrespected	over-controlled
unappreciated	underestimated
unfulfilled	powerless
unchallenged	overworked
unmotivated	underpaid
apathetic	stressed
exploited	judged
bored	replaceable
criticised	unimportant
unsupported	afraid
hindered	insecure

When we have negative feelings we are more:

critical	non-accepting
aggressive	disapproving
judgemental	impatient
closed-minded	inflexible

Problems caused by negative feelings are:

- increase in defensiveness
- increase in staff turnover and consequent loss of skills
- absenteeism
- lost work time
- inefficient communication
- dishonesty, secrecy, evasiveness
- decrease in creativity
- fear of risk-taking, criticism, judgement and disapproval
- inefficient problem solving
- increased personal attacks

Case study: client in the financial services sector

A study of an organisation's culture looked at the relationship with customers in order to design a Customer Focus Programme (CFP) strategy. This had to start with the leadership team having greater insight to its own dynamics. Questions were explored such as:

1. Is your leadership team greater than the sum of its parts?
2. Is your leadership team simply a forum for the exchange of information between independent managers?
3. Are there personal conflicts to address, perspectives missed or neglected?
4. Do your leaders speak with a common vision and understanding to the rest of you?

The findings were as follows:

- Their values should be more closely aligned with reality by examining their espoused values as well as instigating some high-profile changes in the visible areas.
- Research and reviews of the visible areas and values/assumptions should be ongoing.

- Values-led behaviour should be labelled as an aspiration (not actual) where appropriate.
- Senior managers particularly should be targeted to bring about cultural change in their areas. Inclusion of cultural issues would be useful into management practices, discussion and action at appraisals, performance management meetings and team meetings.
- Specific influential departments should be targeted for action on cultural change.
- Performance Management and CFP should be introduced to Head Office not just branches.
- Findings of cultural research and successes in bringing about cultural change should be shared widely through briefings and training programmes.
- All current and future projects should include cultural change goals.
- The day-to-day model must be one of respecting the individual so that the contribution includes initiatives as well as the core job; the team creates innovation in its 'business engine'.
- The leader must show fairness across the team.
- When evaluating ideas for implementation, there must be demonstrable respect for the idea, the individual and the broader consequences for the team.

There was a low degree of self-awareness amongst the leadership team, and so the CFP programme had to start with the leaders taking stock and recognising the emotional roots of behaviour. Simple behavioural changes resulted in improved income within three months of the programme. For example, a senior manager met with and actively listened to his female part-time staff and as a direct result of experiencing their feelings being heard, more products were sold over the counter than ever achieved before. The extra income generated from one employee of a CFP delegate paid for the entire programme for 50 colleagues. Small changes can have a huge impact.

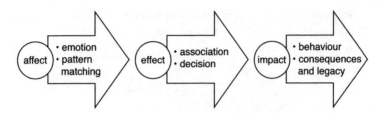

Figure 2.3: The chain of emotions linking to a response

We experience emotions as a response to stimuli (real world events) and whether they threaten us or are pleasant experiences. We test the incoming information against patterns from our past. The effect these have on us is based on any association we can make with them (for example, 'this was dangerous last time', or 'I found this pleasing before'). A decision is made which is most often a sub-conscious one and we act in response. The response is observed as behaviour which may have short-term consequences and possibly a longer term legacy which can be to our benefit or to our cost.

Our bodies inform us of key pieces of information which can tell us what path to take – this is human intuition. Yet we fight some basic principles which are generally evident to us from early adulthood.

A few principles

- All humans have basic emotional needs.
- Each of us has similar, but different emotional needs.
- Emotional needs vary more in degree than in type.
- Emotional needs vary more than physical needs.
- Emotional needs are more basic and more important than 'rights'.
- Negative feelings are indications of our unmet emotional needs (UENs).

- Feelings are real and are not debatable.
- Invalidation destroys self-esteem.
- High self-esteem is needed for productivity, job satisfaction, and customer service.
- Group harmony requires both mutual need satisfaction and mutual respect of feelings.

Consider how these principles might apply to your everyday life.

Who should fix the problem?

Learning occurs whether we like it or not.

This means that bad learning occurs at work when employees see managers breaking their promises or going against espoused values. When faced with problems at work it may seem easy for us to feel that we are not in control and that things just happen to us. Phrases come to our mind such as 'It's not my fault' or 'They should do something about this.'

The organisation is responsible for bad learning experiences that will go on where learning is not overtly on the agenda in everyday operations.

learning experience	positive	negative
own performance and productivity	stimulated to greater performance and productivity	impacts motivation negatively leading to apathy and strain
reputation	enhanced	damaged
relationship	improves and deepens	leads to upset or breaks

Table 2.2: Learning experience outcomes

The consequences are not always felt immediately, such as when the response is one of withdrawal leading to sabotage and rebellious passive-aggressive behaviour.

However, a more positive view would recognise that we all contribute, to some extent, to what is happening around us. Our contribution may be from something that we do quite often, or from what we do not do. It may be that fears or worries of some kind have held us back from taking action: fear of a confrontation, perhaps, or worries about our ideas being wrong.

If we take a more positive view we can often find ways in which we can change an unsatisfactory situation for the better. We need to substitute negativity with positive phrases such as: *'I can improve this situation by …'.*

Some of the events you have recalled in reviewing your learning experiences may well have been totally out of your control, but there is likely to be at least one to which you have contributed. It is possible to start with simple behaviours, such as saying 'yes' more when hearing ideas without overly exercising the manager's right of veto. If you are fair you can be firm in weeding out weak ideas.

Equally the terminology we use can be heard more effectively if we learn about the communication style preferences of those with whom we work.

Approval-seeking behaviour

One of the underlying reasons for non-assertive behaviour may be that we have high need for the approval of other people. We all like to be liked, but for some people that need to be liked overrides other needs. Sometimes the approval that we then receive is not enough to compensate us for not having satisfied our other needs; we may end up feeling 'put-upon'.

To help you identify the origin of any needs you may have for the approval of others, and to identify the advantages and drawbacks of meeting such needs, try and identify at least three situations from your past where you learned to seek the approval of others. One typical example might be from a parent reacting to your behaviour with a message such as, 'People don't like little boys or girls who do that.'

Try to identify examples of situations at work where you behave so as to seek the approval of others. Examples might be:

- staying late because your boss disapproves of people who go home on time
- always volunteering for the nasty job that nobody likes doing.

What are the disadvantages to you of such approval-seeking behaviour? What do you lose by it? Examples could be:

- the respect of colleagues
- the opportunity to do other things you would rather do.

Alternative behaviours

Consider the disadvantages in relation to the benefits of other people's approval. If you believe that you are paying a high price for such approval, what could you do?

What action could you take to reduce your approval-seeking behaviour? Examples could be:

- being prepared to carry out a task without first getting agreement
- being willing to state your own opinions and feelings before everyone else expresses theirs.

Make a mental note of the occasions when you do or say things primarily to seek other people's approval.

EI is learnable

Raising EQ is possible because EI is learnable. Modern neuroscience tells us that the emotional centre of the brain learns differently than the cognitive centre. We can learn to fine-tune, or increase our use of, different parts of the human brain.

Remember what it was like when you first learned to drive a car? You did not know what you did not know. Do you remember how the way you were treated affected your ability to retain the lessons and your self-confidence? Alternatively, do you remember changing cars and having to retrain yourself to switch on the lights without having to think where the switch was? Getting to do these things at the 'unconscious competence' level involves building a new neural pathway in your brain.

You will know if you need to find out more about how you learn best. What ways of learning do you find most helpful? If you do not know how to explore your learning preferences, set up a period of enquiry. Your preferred learning style may be to engage in immediate activity more than pausing to reflect. However, rounding off learning styles to take on different methods is good development in processing information and problem analysis in itself. If you stick to your natural one or two styles of learning you may miss out (see Figure 2.4).

When you get emotionally hijacked

Remember 'the tiger in your tent' in Chapter 1? Let's look at what happened. Your reaction is an instantaneous adrenaline-based

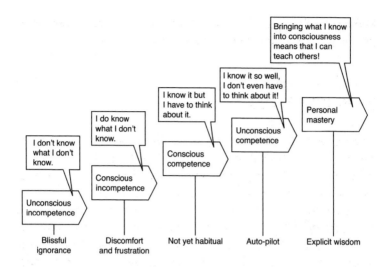

Figure 2.4: The stages of learning

reaction and has no cognition associated with it. It is an emotional hijack because the second brain processes reactions some 80,000 times faster than the neocortex processes thoughts (the third brain).

How can we take advantage of this faster processing? The greater speed is beneficial when we use it to make better decisions using wide-ranging sources of data: soft (emotional, intuitive) information as well as the traditional hard (cognitive, knowledge) data. It is powerful when we pick up information from all our senses and use it more perceptively to manage physiology, relationships and social situations.

> 'The ancient brain centres for emotion also harbour the skills needed for managing ourselves effectively and for social adeptness. Thus these skills are grounded in our evolutionary heritage for survival and adaptation.'
> Daniel Goleman, *Working with Emotional Intelligence*
> (Bloomsbury Publishing, 1998)

Implications in a business environment

You are likely to have had several close-call situations causing an adrenaline rush in your day-to-day work life. For example, when the boss says, 'I want to see you in my office in five minutes,' your body is primed for action and is reacting with the fight reactions of anger, aggression and hostility or the flight/freeze emotions of fear, anxiety and nervousness. It is stressful not to be able to release the fight or flight energy provided, through expected physical activity. This lack of release causes many illnesses. Do we carefully consider all of the reasons why our boss wishes to see us? No, we immediately assume we are in trouble and panic. This reaction was developed appropriately for situations encountered by Early Man when physically threatened. Today, there are generally fewer threats to our personal safety. The main threats that we perceive are of a financial, emotional, mental and social nature. These types of threats are constantly present in our environment and are not generally dealt with immediately.

How will developing EI change me?
I have direct experience of a year-long emotional intelligence development programme in my own company:

- It has changed me and how I am interpersonally for the better.
- I am able to bear much greater stress and take more risks than I could before with much reduced anxiety.
- It has changed how we are as a team for the better.
- It has increased the advocacy, referrals and quality of testimonials that we receive from clients.
- It has improved how we communicate with suppliers and deal with complaints.
- It has helped us to set achievable goals that align our personal lives with business ambitions.

Keeping a journal

Raising your EQ to reduce and eliminate unproductive behaviour is rarely completed in one step. Development of any kind is difficult with low self-awareness; something which is notoriously difficult to train. It has to be part of a developmental process over a period of time usually following a pattern of input, reflection and discovery.

It is useful to keep a journal to log your learning. Keep the journal in one place so it is readily to hand. Use it to prepare for meetings, noting your feelings, thoughts or expectations of the event.

Make a record of experiences and situations you have encountered whilst the memory is fresh. This will give you the benefit of higher quality reflection. Stick to keeping the journal – remember it takes three weeks to form a good habit. I keep a single book including my work notes as well. At least once a year, I review the content tabbing up the pages. I write up my conclusions, plus any follow-up activity in my latest journal. Often I find little gems of advice I missed.

Journal format

Your journal chronicles your steps on your journey of discovery and self-development. General rules are to:

- Date the entry giving qualitative details of the environment and experience.
- Give some context (why you are where you are and with whom). Give anything relevant about the timing such as an appraisal interview.
- Note anything that distracts you (you may be participating in a meeting, listening to a presentation or giving a coaching session, etc).

- Note anything that interferes with your relationship(s) with other participants and with your role (chairperson, coach, etc).

What additional EI competences are required to be an effective manager?

Organisations pay for behaviour at work – obviously they want that behaviour to carry out a role, deliver planned outputs and further the organisation in terms of improvements. An effective manager is able to get staff to go the extra mile. If the team are well managed they will share initiatives with their colleagues. It is initiative sharing and the way the organisation processes these ideas that leads to innovation and organisational learning.

The way you behave with your customers creates a better sensation for them than they would experience with the competition, and thus gives you the advantage. Success in sustaining this is generated from within each individual – in the way they treat themselves, in their dealings with colleagues and in their relationships with internal customers in the business.

Each organisation is unique and the competitive advantage which can be generated uniquely determines and makes a difference to your future, so review your operation along the following lines:

Competitive advantage

- No more guesswork, pinpoint hotspots using performance measurement.
- Highlight strengths within your team and target solutions.
- Define outcomes with measurable results.

- Make organisational and individual recommendations for improvements.
- Compare your management performance with others like you.
- Highly customise your solutions to maintain client energy levels.
- Focus on your uniqueness.

Adaption and innovation

You, as a manager, need to be able to inspire innovation and see it through into serving customers as an operational reality. You need to be good at problem-solving and using the different talents in the team to come up with innovations that are robust and tested ideas. How do you measure this as a basis for team-building and designing your processes to innovate and problem-solve?

The Kirton Adaption-Innovation (KAI) Inventory

This is an inventory that measures an individual's preferred cognitive style (i.e. the processes that lead to a successful manifestation of creativity, problem-solving and decision-making). It is a useful language in which to explain differences in working practices and comfort levels, especially in relation to the need for structure. It enables individuals to see how they differ in the way they approach, define and solve problems.

The inventory measures people on their style of problem-solving and creativity. The measure is used:

- in the training of managers and key teams as part of the management of change
- in group training and individual development as part of the management of diversity

- for the enhancement of group cohesion and effectiveness
- for leadership development
- for team building in problem-solving together.

The KAI indicates whether one has a preference as an adaptor or innovator; those with scores higher than 96 are considered innovators; lower scores than 96 indicate an adaptor. Kirton's definition of an innovator is a person who is 'less tolerant of structure (guidelines, rules) and who is less respectful of consensus'. An innovator will break rules and paradigms to produce a new way of doing things.

An adaptor has more respect for rules and structure. He or she prefers to solve problems in a defined environment, working to do things 'better' as opposed to breaking the paradigms.

While the adaptor thrives on structure and has a penchant for order, predictability and repeatability, the innovator seeks newness and experimentation, fails to see structure or credits structural consistency as contributing to the problem. Kirton is careful to point out that this scale does not mean adaptors are not creative. They can be as equally creative as innovators but the way they solve problems is different.

People with KAI scores of more than ten points apart will notice a difference in problem-solving methodology. People with KAI scores more than twenty points apart may have difficulty understanding each other's point of view.

Innovators and adaptors can create anxiety for each other, and the further the reported preference favours one or the other, the more potential for friction. KAI is particularly useful with teams, making clear to each member the range of diversity (including style) that needs to be understood and well used for the benefit of the whole team. The team needs to know and share openly the vital value of such diversity managed well. Such management, Kirton argues, underlies all successful resolution of the many, complex problems that successful teams need to master.

Being an effective manager

'Individuals and teams learn best when a climate is created that *supports* the *quality* of time at work rather than the output.'

(Honda, 1998)

Often the 'command and control model' of managing people stifles their innovation at work. The factors that contribute to an effective organisation are the ability to capture those experiences that give *life* to the individual in private/social life and the ability to transfer them to the workplace. Moments of creative peaks occur when individuals or teams are separated from their thoughts and feelings as people, in addition to what they do.

- Implicit and tacit *wisdom* in every organisation becomes active when it resonates in the same way in each member of a team.
- Learning takes place when what is created between organisational teams and individuals is made manifest and real, and is spoken about and acted upon.
- Individuals will recycle the learning stages as their relationship with the organisation becomes more intimate.
- Our ability to learn is also gained by positive and negative experiences of education and these can be revisited at work.

People will gravitate towards peers and managers who most replicate *good* learning experiences (they become referents regardless of their place in the pecking order). Organisational learning succeeds when this is most valued and a positive climate is created to accommodate it.

In order to maintain organisational learning principles and practice, people must be educated both in what learning means and how good learning occurs for them. This should be embedded into the induction processes. Of note and for consideration is the point that few organisations today can exist with a resource strategy of 100 per cent permanent employee status; it is the norm to co-exist with different kinds of human resource suppliers. Therefore, *the (mainly induction)* needs of long-term consultants, temporary staff and partner organisation/strategic alliance staff need to be reviewed and provided for in addition. This is to maintain a single, integral culture in the internal as well as external customer relationships. There is a business case for this investment.

Excellence is picked up when the core competence is cycled around a team and discriminating competence in individuals is observed and identified in such a way that it can be transferred to others. Good team managers can do this. Others can be taught how. There is a continuous renewal of the core competence as previously discriminating ability is added to the core and thus the bar of performance is raised.

Effective managers:

- are willing to hold up the mirror and continuously assess their own performance against changing organisational needs
- identify how to raise the bar of core competence on a continuous improvement basis
- identify learning in the individual, team and organisation which requires expression and discussion in order to add value to work practice; thus bad learning experiences are correctly processed and good learning experiences are shared all round.

How do you know someone is an effective manager? Ask staff how they feel around this person. Key feelings to track are: I feel respected, controlled, criticised, supported, appreciated, relaxed or judged.

Let us look at a domestic scenario and draw some parallels with the manager at work. A father is observing the behaviour of his children and is assigning motives to it without checking out his assumptions. His behaviour is about punishing the children and admonishing them for what is perceived as unacceptable. The children feel a sense of injustice and unrequited anger at his treatment of them and they are told not to speak when they want to discuss it. The breakdown in the relationship leads to a model of critical parent and rebellious child. If the harassed mother arrives and takes the side of the father, then what is left in the children's emotional bank account is:

- she didn't listen
- she took sides without hearing from me
- she didn't believe me
- she was unfair.

Draw some parallels with this at work. Have there been incidents where people did not take responsibility for behaviour that was damaging in some way? Remember, at work, adults can be ruled by the five-year-old inside.

Summary

1. Start talking about feelings.
2. Start respecting them.
3. Start assigning value to them.
4. Include feelings in decision-making and problem resolution.
5. Listen to the most sensitive people in the organisation.
6. Strike a balance between emotion and logic.
7. Develop EQ skills throughout the organisation.
8. Prohibit invalidation.
9. Make your business a place of mutual respect for feelings.

10. Identify the key feelings important for success.
11. Establish feeling goals for employees and customers.
12. Use a simple scale such as 0–10 to track feelings.

INSTANT TIP

Build your own business case for personal change. Learn from it and share it with those you manage.

03

How do I get some EI?

How is EI developed?

Curiosity is a wonderful thing. Human beings can grow their self-awareness by being curious about themselves, their inner selves and their impact on the world around them. There are two basic types of learning and it is an important distinction for EI development purposes:

- cognitive
- emotional

Cognitive learning is about absorbing new data and insights into existing frameworks of association and understanding. For example, if a manufacturing unit is upgraded following redesign, you have to learn all of the features, advantages and benefits of the upgrade in order to sell it to clients. Emotional learning involves absorbing new self-knowledge and insights into an existing self-identity with a more profound understanding of relationships and more. Emotional learning involves engaging that part of the brain where our emotional signature is stored (in the second brain or limbic system).

As with IQ, everyone has a starting basis across the EQ scale but the good news is that you can raise your EQ through development. Emotional learning involves changing habits such as:

- learning to approach people positively rather than avoiding them when a sales relationship is at risk
- listening effectively to clients – not being silent only as a pause before you speak, but actively listening with empathic communication designed to first gain understanding of the client or prospect before seeking to transmit a sales message
- giving feedback skilfully, for example, if you need a client to understand why a project did not go as planned due to a failure on their side of the customer/supplier interface.

Emotional learning is much more challenging than simply adding new data to old (cognitive learning). Emotional learning involves new ways of thinking and acting that are more in tune with our identity – our values, beliefs and attitudes. If you are told to learn a new sales order processing programme, you will probably get on with it. However, if you are told that you need to improve control of your mood, you are likely to be upset or offended.

So the prospect of needing to develop greater Emotional Intelligence is likely to generate resistance to change. We will therefore have to address your ability to change, to form new habits by learning emotionally and to accept attitudinal shifts and new frames of reference. This 'learning about learning' is in addition to specific emotional competency development.

Methods of supervision in EI development

Other important distinctions in learning are the methods of supervision by which you learn best:

- working with a coach, one to one
- working with a mentor, one to one
- working with a facilitator at a group event addressing change issues
- being led by a supervisor through a change process.

The first line of management has the most influence over a workforce. A change programme needs to take this into account in order to embed organisational change messages, to unfreeze the status quo and to identify what is required and make the transition. In a climate where the first-line supervisor is unlikely to achieve this then another form of supervision is required, e.g. coach, mentor or facilitator.

Levels of supervision

There are six levels of supervision:

1. reflecting on the current task to be undertaken
2. exploration of the strategies and tasks to be carried out
3. exploration of the personal relationship
4. focus upon the individual's response to the task in progress
5. focus upon the relationship between the mentor and individual as a direct reflection of the need to be addressed (interpersonal only).
6. focus upon the mentor's response to the process.

Human beings are adaptive and positive emotions or characteristics can be adopted as 'new habits'. It used to be thought that the brain takes 21 days to form a fresh habit, a new neural pathway. However, the process is actually more complex. If we think of it simplistically initially, then the process is like a new pathway being beaten into a jungle and an old trail being no longer trodden down. The flora and fauna would reclaim it.

Gentle	Doing nothing	
	Silence	
	Support	
	Questions to clarify	Supportive
	Questions to change	_____
Intervention Style	Questions to move	
	Suggesting choices	
	Suggesting paths	Persuasive
	Sharing ideas	
	Suggesting action	_____
Forceful	Guidance	
	Deciding choice for group	Directive
	Directing	

Figure 3.1: The facilitation spectrum

Equally, an old bad habit must be consistently abandoned to lose its power as a tendency (for the neural pathways of habitual behaviour to die off). Sometimes on a new pathway another old one intersects the path we are on and this leads us back, via an alternative route, to the bad habit which was in the process of being discarded. Should we weaken and follow it the behaviour is reinforced, the bad habit becomes customary again.

Such are the somatic markers in our brain, that patterns or chains of emotions remind us of some comfortable past behaviour, and we slip back from the new good habit to the old. We have failed to be resilient through the *conscious incompetence* stage of the learning ladder and sustain the *conscious competence* level.

Sometimes to form new good habits, we have to create our own climate of positive affirmation. This includes:

● the ability to self-audit and for this personal development to be valued at work
● to be in a non-judgemental environment of evaluation (where discoveries are used for growth and not the criticism of the individual)

- to be able to grow your own fun-based toolkit where experimentation and exploration are possible
- to be where you can use your innate gifts such as mood control to shift energy and enthusiasm.

You will have seen that the human body is healthier when it resides for the majority of the time with positive emotions: gratitude or appreciation of others, optimism, zest for life or being dynamic. It has been found that in addition, curiosity and the ability to love and be loved are vital to living a highly satisfied life.

Cognitive skills are called 'hard' skills, while those associated with emotional intelligence are called 'soft'. This idea has been enshrined through the ages. Only through understanding what occasionally triggers unproductive behaviour (low EQ) can we determine self-knowledge as a basis for change.

Three stages of insight

Hindsight:	I wish I had said that instead of ... or I wish I had done that instead of ...
Middlesight:	What is happening now? (Sometimes I am not in control of my thinking on the spot.)
Foresight:	Knowing how I need to behave in advance to manage the emotional climate of a given situation or what to try beforehand.

A five-step plan to manage feelings

1. identify the primary feelings
2. identify the cause of the feelings
3. ask what would help (me/you) feel better?

4. generate options
5. choose the best option.

Revisiting a mildly distressing situation

This may not sound like a lot of fun but it has enormous value. By mentally re-experiencing a difficult or mildly painful experience, you learn more about how you react emotionally to situations and you cause the emotion to seem less formidable. Do not use this for serious issues requiring professional help from a counsellor or qualified medical adviser.

We are often reluctant to get in touch with distressing emotions, yet those are usually the ones from which we can learn the most. It is useful to understand how we can tap into those emotions. Here's a way for learning to do that.

- Pick a quiet time and space. Bring into focus the mildly distressing situation. Close your eyes. Call up in your mind the experience that caused you to feel a strong emotion.
- Try to reconstruct the setting as clearly as you can. This helps you get in touch with the emotions better. Suppose an authority figure called you into their office, saying they wanted to talk with you. You went in and sat down. You could see the rain pouring off the university building's rooftop. You saw the photos of the children on his desk. You could hear the traffic coming and going outside. You were sitting on an uncomfortable plastic chair.
- Try to reconstruct the conversation: 'Janine, I have to tell you that your output is considerably below the other people's in your group. You know we're in a real drive to get all assignments complete before Easter. I don't know what's going on with you, but I'd certainly like you to tell

me, because if you can't do the study, I've got a long list of people who want your place.'
- Try to re-experience the emotions you felt during that encounter. The shame at having your work put down and your abilities questioned. The anger at the person's unreasonableness (your assignment was much more complicated than those of other people in the group). The terror that you would lose your university place and not find another, and you and your family would be humiliated.
- Ask yourself if your emotions seemed appropriate. The terror was probably an overreaction (you didn't really believe your tutor would replace you). The shame was unnecessary (you were actually quite convinced that you worked as hard as anyone could have, given the circumstances).

By trying exercises such as this, we can begin to connect with the emotional roots of our behaviour and new choices in any given situation will present themselves. This way you can turn the times when you act with foresight and not hindsight to be more frequent.

What additional competencies are involved in the acquisition of EI capability?

The additional competencies involved in the acquisition of EI capability are:

- learning styles (preferences)
- self-directed learning (competence) and being coachable
- perception and ability to think 'outside the box'.

If you have never completed an assessment of your preferred learning styles, then it would be helpful to do so before undertaking Emotional Intelligence development.

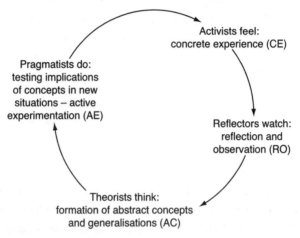

Kolb's learning cycle is a continuum and no one position processes learning comprehensively to the exclusion of all others

Activists feel:
concrete experience (CE)

Pragmatists do:
testing implications
of concepts in new
situations – active
experimentation (AE)

Reflectors watch:
reflection and
observation (RO)

Theorists think:
formation of abstract concepts
and generalisations (AC)

Figure 3.2: Kolb's learning cycle

The four different styles when employed will provide an individual, team and organisation with robust solutions when problem-solving and making decisions. Developing EI requires experiential emotional learning and the 'reflector' learning style for the lessons to endure beyond a single event. This emotional learning may be different from the education, training and development that you have experienced before now. The reason for this is illustrated in the diagram on self-directed learning (see Figure 3.5). EI is an awareness-based method of learning. Objective feedback is essential and therefore it is highly compatible with 360-degree feedback assessments from staff and peers, as well as feedback through other relationships such as through skilled questioning from a coach. The individual has to accept that the answers come from within and are not given to them. It is important that the answers are not 'given answers'.

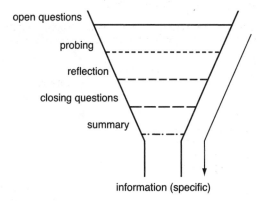

Figure 3.3: The questioning funnel

There is a danger once self-awareness is raised that individuals fall into denial, being so challenged by the discoveries about themselves. This results in avoidance of action altogether and individuals can withdraw/disengage in a number of ways. Even if you do not like change you are probably developing ways of coping with it. You may recognise one of the following coping strategies:

- you insist that the old way is better and safer
- you accept the change but only once someone else has made the effort to persuade you
- you immediately accept it at face value because it's new
- you initiate the change yourself to control it
- you thrive on it!
- you pretend that it is not happening.

Elizabeth Kübler-Ross developed the following model through her work with people undergoing change. The Kübler-Ross change curve helps us identify where we get stuck emotionally.

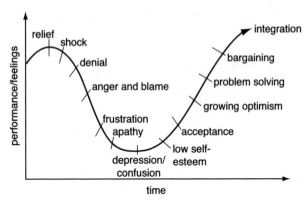

Figure 3.4: Typical feelings during times of uncertainty

How do you cope with change? Do you recognise any of the stages (which are not always processed sequentially) on the Kübler-Ross Change Curve?

There is no knowledge transfer to become one's ideal self in self-directed learning. There has to be a self-audit that is non-judgemental (no telling yourself off). You have to give yourself permission to be your ideal self. You have to practise, practise, practise. There are many exercises such as meditation, clearing, visualisation and anchoring which can fast-track this ideal self becoming the real you; you can be creative and have some fun too.

Mechanics of the emotional radar

When you have a reasonable degree of Emotional Intelligence, you recognise that in any situation you are equally capable of being the 'difficult person' from another's point of view. If managed constructively, as in the Myers-Briggs Type Indicator (MBTI) view

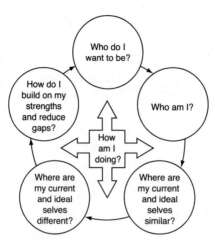

Figure 3.5: Self-directed learning

of 'gifts differing', you recognise that if managed constructively, different gifts aid and result in creativity. Adaptation is how we have survived several million years, so our emotional radar has developed (in the 'tribe of man') to:

1. watch for those not contributing
2. ensure that the diversity is utilised from whatever source (background, perspective, expertise, experience, knowledge and skill-base)
3. manage those whose contributions overawe other team members
4. watch for inappropriate competitiveness where collaboration and co-operation are more productive
5. inspire initiative-sharing – diverging and then converging to brainstorm ideas and create action plans.

The above are typical qualities used by skilled chairpersons for managing volunteers or attendees of organisational events.

Neural mechanics at work

In order to establish skilled emotional competence, there needs to be a high degree of use of intuition and visceral feedback. This allows you to spring the trap of denial and avoidance of action.

> 'Neuroscience has discovered that our brain's very design makes it sociable, inexorably drawn into an intimate brain-to-brain link-up whenever we engage with another person. That neural bridge lets us affect the brain – and so the body – of everyone we interact with, just as they do us.'
> Daniel Goleman *Social Intelligence*
> (Arrow Books, 2006)

In terms of the rational and irrational, Descartes went as far as to say, 'I think, therefore I am.' In Descartes' view, you needed your hard skills to *override* your soft side in order to make a rational decision. Antonio Damasio, Professor of Neurology at Iowa University, disagrees. One could say equally, 'I feel, therefore I am.' In his book *Descartes' Error*, Damasio's complex theory explains that the physical processes of logic and emotion are closely tied in the brain, arguing that it doesn't make sense to separate the two – affect (feeling) and cognition (thinking).

In practice, we use emotional information as well as logical analysis when we decide what to do. Damasio talks of 'somatic markers' in the brain. These are signals that tell us the likely effects of our intended action. These somatic markers remind us when something is likely to cause more upset than the value of the action warrants. Some professions rely on these 'somatic markers' such as when submarine boat captains, with no visual reference, rely on their 'gut feel' to make critical decisions.

Damasio has worked with patients in whom these cerebral connections have been severed. These individuals are often capable of solving complex logical problems in the clinic, but cannot function socially in the real world. Their decisions take no account of emotional factors. The most extreme example of this predates Damasio.

In 1848, a young man called Phineas Gage was in an explosives accident that resulted in him having an iron bolt impact and penetrate his skull. Astonishingly, this had little effect on his logic, but severed a connection between his neocortex and the limbic system, ruining his ability to do any job where he had to relate to people. The bolt had effectively left his IQ intact but had destroyed his emotional connections.

In the mid-1970s, a Chief Aircrewman working in SeaKing helicopters in England received a piece of avionics shrapnel in his brain in a serious aviation accident. He apparently recovered physically and was able to function technically in his role. However, he lost his sense of humour totally. He was no longer able to function socially in the aircrew culture where a sharp and caustic sense of humour aided survival in high-risk jobs. Whilst flying, reliance on others for survival is a daily norm. His ability to gain a perspective on daily incidents was hampered by an inability to find human frailties the least bit amusing. Feeling pleasure and amusement to reduce fear hijacking your cognitive reasoning is an emotional competence. Emotional factors are relevant to organisational culture.

Perceptions and reality

At every moment of the day all our senses are bombarded by huge quantities of information, so vast that we cannot possibly pay attention to all of it. Necessarily our minds have to focus upon that which appears relevant to us. Our mind filters all the information and directs our attention to what it believes is most important or relevant to us. All of this happens out of our conscious awareness; it is a job done by our 'out-of-awareness' **unconscious** mind. Look at the following picture and notice how your mind automatically takes the incomplete image and makes some sense of it (you should see a dog like a black Labrador). Our mind fills in the blanks and jumps to a conclusion. We do this all the time and it happens out of conscious control.

To illustrate that perception happens out of awareness just try the following simple experiment below. Look steadily at the line drawing and focus on the round spot on the centre line. Notice how you first see the 3D effect one way and then in another. Notice that this change in perception 'happens to you'; you do not consciously decide to see the picture in any particular way.

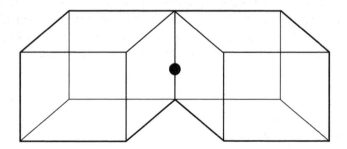

Our unconscious minds arrive at our perceptions for us. What appears to happen is that our unconscious mind very rapidly sifts through all the incoming information compares it with our vast database of life experiences, makes the best sense of it that it can and passes its most important conclusions to our conscious mind.

Our perceptions are a product of our life experiences and the beliefs, values and attitudes that have developed in our minds. They are how we see and experience the world. It is no exaggeration to say that our perceptions literally are our reality. They are the psychological world that we inhabit.

It is also the case that if a person believes something to be true, he or she will act as if it is true.

Implications for management and communications

Since each person's experiences, beliefs, values and attitudes are unique to them, we each live in different psychological realities. No two people are likely to perceive the same situation in exactly the same way. The implications of these differences are immense. This has special relevance for managers of people.

You can of course question your perceptions, but to do so requires continuous proactive questioning. Unless we do this we tend to perceive people, their behaviours and situations in specific ways, to take our perceptions as if they are facts and act as if they are true. Hence there is huge potential for miscommunication.

Why is Emotional Intelligence important?

Most people spend more time than they would like thinking about when they lost control or misunderstood others. To mature and to be congruent in the company of others, we each have to connect with our inner selves and our uniqueness.

A high Intelligence Quotient (IQ) is not enough to guarantee success in life. When you have a high Emotional Intelligence Quotient (EQ) you are adept at interpreting the emotional roots to your own thinking and behaviour and *choosing* your actions to influence outcomes. You are also capable of making good insights into the behaviour of others.

We all know that changing behaviour in a sustained and genuine way is extremely difficult. Change Agents need both a high EQ and practical techniques for dealing with others when stressed by change issues.

Improvement cannot be achieved solely by attending a training course or reading a book to acquire knowledge. Skills associated with emotional intelligence develop throughout life. Training and sustained development activity at work can improve emotional competence.

How will developing my own EI affect me personally?

A manager who develops their EI will have recognisable benefits at home and at work.

Evidence of high EQ

- We are clear, flexible and collaborative about changing priorities.
- We reach targets with greater ease and less stress.
- We are focused, efficient and are cool under pressure.
- We are elated, not tired, and satisfied at the end of the day.
- We have a great work/life balance.
- We are dynamic, have energy and humour.
- We look younger than our age.

Example of high EQ

Think for a moment of one example where you have had a positive emotional response to how well you were handled, for example:

- face-to-face with a sales assistant in a shop
- in the past when an authority figure had to give you some bad news but with a more positive outcome for you
- by e-mail or a telephone conversation that left you feeling inspired, with a glow and motivated.

Personal outcomes of low EQ

Here are some examples:

- We are worried, anxious or confused about priorities.
- We are time-pressured, inefficient and perform poorly.
- We are tired, fatigued and frustrated.

- We have a poor work/life balance.
- We may have poor health, especially elevated blood pressure.
- We age more quickly.

Clearly, these are outcomes which are best avoided by raising our EQ.

How will developing my own EI at work help me?

Managers who aspire to further develop their EQ are likely to encounter nothing but encouragement from their staff and peers. Developing Emotional Intelligence is more than raising our self-awareness and self-knowledge. It involves knowing, understanding and accepting our strengths and weaknesses. To be effective managers we need:

- self-knowledge
- an accurate self-identity backed up by 360-degree feedback from those with whom we work
- insight into our preferred styles of thinking
- to be conscious of our values and goals particularly when espoused values are compromised by actual behaviour
- essentially, to understand and be happy with our place in the world.

Self-disclosure

Self-disclosure is being yourself, recognising and owning your opinions, values and feelings and understanding that these are no more valid than anyone else's. We can share these with others, remembering that they are only our map of the territory of our mind and are perceptions.

You may feel comfortable with many of your own characteristics and less happy about others. To self-manage effectively, you need to be aware of your optimum stress levels and the ways in which you cope, as well as knowing your goals and the values that guide you.

You may well feel better mentally and physically after raising your EQ but it would also be perfectly normal to have lapses back to some unhelpful behaviour. However, you will have better personal insight about why the lapse occurred and be able to prevent a recurrence. People might say you look less stressed or that you do not overreact, and you may feel more grown-up or at peace with yourself.

'If you always do what you have always have done, then you will always get what you have always got.'

Leadership potential

1. In your current team, what are your main leadership challenges?
2. Who wants what from you and what do you want from yourself?
3. Evaluate and group them where relevant.
4. How do members of staff perceive you as their leader? (What would they say to you?)
5. If you developed your EQ, what would have the biggest impact on your leadership?
6. What are the obstacles to achieving this?
7. How would you overcome these obstacles?

Share the results of your thinking with a colleague and compare ideas.

Summary

Reflect on:

1. What I think EI is and how it affects me.
2. What low EQ looks like and what the consequences are for me of low EQ behaviour.
3. What high EQ looks like and the benefits that can be reaped by me.
4. Who has been a good role model for me?
5. What leadership challenges I face.
6. What my staff may think of me in EI terms.
7. What I want to concentrate on to become more emotionally intelligent.

INSTANT TIP

When you wake up tomorrow morning start by saying: 'How am I going to *be* today?' *Then* think about your schedule and list of things to do.

04

How do I apply EI?

Is EI just a fad?

The people who promote EI are not talking about anything new. Emotional and social intelligence has been discussed since the 1920s. We have all known about the importance of interpersonal skills and having positive attitudes for some time now. Emotional Intelligence includes Intrapersonal Intelligence as well as interpersonal intelligence and therefore self-management as well as relationship management. It also includes the deeper levels of our values and attitudes and is not just about skills and competencies. Soft-skills training is familiar to businesses but having a hard financial case for developing these has been lacking until now. What has been less familiar to the business world is the importance of intrapersonal skills, like the capacity to tolerate stress, mood and impulse control and the capacity for empathy.

Is Emotional Intelligence just personality measures dressed up? Personality variables are predispositions which by definition are relatively unchanging (not impossible however) whereas all Emotional Intelligence components are open to change.

Why choose to develop it? This is an easy one to answer because there are so many areas of life that having high EQ improves. For example, it helps you in all your working relationships, whether horizontal or vertical. Although you can be born with a higher or lower potential in either intrapersonal or interpersonal intelligence you can improve them both significantly at any age.

- Having high EQ makes you a superior performer. This is shown clearly by the research on performance and EQ.
- People with high EQ are optimistic and realistic. They tend to envisage good outcomes, which they then make happen.
- People with high EQ are far less likely to suffer badly from stress-related illnesses or depression.

The recent development of EQ tests has meant that these aspects are now measurable and with this has come the possibility of developing the capacities they measure and being able to plot the changes and outcomes as the training takes place.

Other reasons why Emotional Intelligence is not just a fad include:

- **Educational research** – in the last 20 years steps forward have been made in defining and understanding the nature of intelligence. Now it is thought that each individual has multiple intelligences and that the emphasis that has been placed on only two of these, the rational/logical and the linguistic, has meant that intelligent and talented individuals have been missed because their intelligence profile did not conform to these two types. Two of the seven currently identified intelligences are interpersonal intelligence and intrapersonal intelligence.
- **Brain research** – brain research has taken big strides in the last ten years with greater knowledge and understanding of the brain function and its

neurophysiology. Now we know more about links and connections in the brain than we did before.

- **Scientific research** – this has demonstrated that decisions cannot be made without reference to the limbic system, which is the emotional centre of the brain. We must be able to tell what we are feeling because without that knowledge we are rudderless.

There are also numerous reasons that make Emotional Intelligence vital to any successful business.

- Globalisation of business has risen and with it so has competition. With increased competition and the faster rate of change through technological advances the need for creativity and flexibility has risen – these are emotionally intelligent traits.
- Bureaucracy and hierarchy in companies have decreased and the need for self and relationship management has got greater.
- Team-working in organisations has increased and with it the need for relationship management skills to cope with the collaborative working methods.
- People can and do move around much more then before and when they leave they take with them a vital asset – knowledge of your company and culture. Considering people as assets that need to stay with a company means that they can be invested in through development programmes. These programmes are no longer limited to technical skills but must encompass the whole person.
- Specialisation is becoming rarer in the work place, particularly in sales and customer service. Now everyone in the company is supposed to be responsible for sales. This means everyone must be emotionally intelligent and strong in interpersonal skills as well as their own role and great at networking to further the business.

● Finally, organisations are flatter by design and this has brought its own brand of stress with an immediate need for self-management techniques.

This is the case for Emotional Intelligence and why it is not just a fad but something to be considered very seriously as one of the few remaining areas in an organisation that can be developed to make a very significant impact on the bottom line.

Business applications of EQ measurement

The main EI schools of thought are:

● The Emotional and Social Competence Inventory (ECSI™) – Boyatzis, Goleman and Hay/McBer
● The BarOn Emotional Quotient Inventory (EQ-i™) – Dr Reuven Bar-On and Dr. Steven Stein
● The EQ Map™ – Advanced Intelligence Technologies & Essi Systems-Orioli, Sawaf, and Cooper
● The Emotional Intelligence Questionnaire (EIQ™) – Dulewicz and Higgs through ASE
● The Multifactor Emotional Intelligence Scale (MEIS™) and the Mayer, Salovey and Caruso EI Test (MSCEIT™).

There are two main areas where EQ measurement and development play a big part in organisations. In both cases it is centred upon the ability EQ has to predict job success and high workplace performance:

1. the selection and recruitment of good candidates
2. the development of existing staff and executives.

Areas where understanding and developing EQ are invaluable include:

- profiling star performers in Emotional Intelligence
- recruitment/selection on the basis of these profiles
- continuing development programmes to attract and keep the best graduate recruits
- identifying and meeting individual, team and organisational development needs
- designing training and evaluation criteria
- individual and teamwork diagnosis
- leadership styles development
- developing outstanding executive leaders.

Case study: Financial impact of high EQ

A bank had serious staff retention issues, particularly with part-time female staff. Rationally, the managers proved unable to make a difference to this loss of staff and failed to incentivise those who remained.

This was independently evaluated and had pleasantly startling results for a relatively modest investment. Every one of the 41 interviewed reported improvements from transformational to specific benefits in self-awareness competencies and improved relationships. Simple changes like listening actively to members of staff rather than being directive with them led to improved sales over the bank counter. Cashiers felt more valued by their manager so they offered customers more products. This was achieved by enhancing the skills of the HR partners and the line managers.

Because of the company's budgetary constraints and limited access to the Internet, we chose to use a different assessment, the EQ Map™ which is self-scored and easy to administer. The facilitation of the event managed any potential misunderstandings about the differences in the models. Stretching them in this fashion gave them a deeper understanding of what EI means in their lives and behaviours regardless of different gurus' opinions or models.

Here are examples how high EQ has had a significant financial impact in organisations:

- **Insurance sales** – sales agents who were relatively weak in EQ competencies such as self-confidence, initiative and empathy sold policies that were worth half the premium value of those sold by colleagues who had strong competencies in at least five out of eight key skills.

- **Executives** – who were recruited by a global consumer beverage company without testing for EQ scores had a turnover of 50 per cent within a two-year period and cost the company $4 million in executive search fees. Once the recruiting policy changed and new candidates were tested for EQ the turnover dropped to 6 per cent.

- **Computer programmers** – those programmers who are in the top 10 per cent of EQ on the scales of willingness to collaborate, disinclination to compete and sharing information out-produce the average programmer by 320 per cent. Those few programmers who are 'star performers' outperform them by 1272 per cent.

These emotional competencies are fundamental in selling, along with the particular competencies of optimism and recovering from setback. The salesperson that knows the product inside out will not succeed without the additional ability to forge strong relationships. To do so the salesperson must win trust, be accurate in their emotional awareness of the client and cope with their own feelings, such as disappointment.

There is plenty of anecdotal evidence that high Emotional Intelligence helps to make sales. People buy from people. If you get on well with customers, they are more likely to buy. There is sound research evidence as well.

As just one example, L'Oreal changed its salespersons' recruitment policy to allow for the emotional competencies of the applicants. The result was a dramatic increase in sales and a corresponding reduction in turnover.

The Hay/McBer Research and Innovation Group compared a group of insurance salespeople who were weak in Emotional Intelligence with another group who were strong in at least five out of eight EI competencies. Using the cold, hard measure of value of sales, the group with better soft skills performed twice as well.

Improving your EQ when working in a group

Before working in a group, look at the outcomes you need as far in advance as possible. Where you can, solicit in advance from other attendees any information on how they regard what needs to be achieved. There is no reason why you cannot explain that you are doing some self-development around how groups could be more valuable. Reflect on your performance at previous events and decide what to work on to raise your self-awareness and self-control.

An example case study if you are stuck...

Faith Brown is a good manager who has been driving herself since May to establish a strong identity in her new role. She lacks self-assurance but is, in fact, immensely capable. Her EQ assessment results and subsequent action planning led her to choose self-confidence, authenticity and flexibility as her developmental edge.

Prepare

Preparation is the main foundation of increasing self-confidence.

- Faith should make sure that she has developed a game plan for the meeting such that she knows when all of the diverse opinions and points have been aired.
- She should prepare for the meeting by committing to be open and honest about particular agenda items and her feelings about them
- She should say confidently what she means and mean what she says authentically.
- During the meeting, she should plan to be resilient to any strongly non-assertive behaviour (aggressive, passive, indirect-aggressive, etc.) from any participant.
- She should make sure that all attendees participate.
- She should conduct the meeting noting mentally any emotional reaction to others' outbursts for later reflection.

Conduct

She should chair the meeting and construct a debate very tightly, so that the diversity of opinion and passions result in a creative outcome. However, participants should not be suppressed such that the meeting ends in an unimaginative compromise with no buy-in.

Reflect

Faith should record and reflect on the results, sharing them as she decides fit. She should plan the next EI development accordingly.

Construct a plan around the agenda items in a real meeting that will allow you to practise greater self-awareness and self-control. Afterwards, reflect on the results:

1. What happened?
2. What are your feelings about it?
3. What went well?
4. What would you do differently?

Self-observations

If after reading these first four chapters you have experienced a short period of developing greater EI competence, ask the following questions in self-study or with a friend or colleague.

1. What was the single most challenging thing about the recent period regarding your behaviour change?
2. What was the easiest thing about the recent period regarding your behaviour change?
3. What did you notice about letting go of old behaviours? Did you want to chuck it in and go back to your old ways?

4. Did you listen to your internal observer when you didn't feel like sticking to it? What did it say?

5. In which situations did you give your power away and not accomplish your goals?

Create a list of times when you are out of routine and you do not perform as you would like in terms of accountability. Treat this as an integrity list – i.e. a list of things that you choose to clear up. It could be:

● relationships
● misconceptions
● assumptions about people or events
● upsets.

INSTANT TIP

Become very conscious of times when you evade being accountable. Think your position through, write down the pros and cons. Identify who is impacted by your evasion of accountability and how they would feel.

05

What benefits do staff get from developing EI?

In determining why EI is important and should be a development priority, we need to look at the personal case for doing so. EI is backed up by a great deal of data and research. We cannot ignore our emotions and the impact they have on our physical and mental health or our everyday lives.

Benefits of 'emotional fitness'

Over the last two decades, many people have tackled their physical fitness and taken charge of their diet to establish a good life balance. People who go to fitness centres, gyms and health spas are generally goal-oriented and want to be more effective. Many people join clubs to feel or look better, follow a beauty regime and to help control their stress. Some have investigated alternative therapies to reduce the impact of stress in their lives. How many have concluded that these are the only solutions to a balanced and healthy life?

Many people stop exercising because they lose motivation. Having to spend 30–40 minutes practising relaxation techniques to wind down at the end of a busy day is very time-consuming. If this is on top of a beauty regime and the gym three to four times a week, it is even more protracted. However, if you are constantly looking after your emotional fitness, it is unnecessary to have to relax to recover from turmoil at work and in your personal life. Prevention is better than cure – always!

EI has been identified as a key factor in:

- beneficial brain chemistry associated with happiness, pleasure and wellbeing
- demonstrable effects on career progression, retention and satisfaction through an investment in Personal Development Plans with Emotional Intelligence competencies
- becoming equipped to set and attain well-rounded outcomes and achieve more ambitious goals.

By implementing in everyday life the programme of development in this book, combined with practical information and guidance on physical fitness, you will gain an understanding of how EI can help to maintain motivation by:

- Improving your interpersonal skills and relationship success by acquiring knowledge, insight and increasing self-awareness. You can apply this to generate energy and vitality in the face of pressures at work and at home.
- Gaining an understanding of how EI development can reduce the 'post-event' effort to relax as well as support stress management strategies that reduce the likelihood of long-term illness.
- Becoming equipped with the basic skills to deconstruct your own behaviour in areas where it is mystifying or unhelpful and to generate foresight rather than hindsight about your behaviour.
- Gaining an understanding of the mind–body link and those factors that contribute to your emotional wellbeing.

Through a combination of the above, you can generate a new way of being in the 21st century and save yourself some time.

Your personal window on the world and your place in it

Feedback

Feedback is a subjective process which is managed objectively in most organisations. Feedback is about getting to know other people's 'map of the world' – their opinions, values, experiences, expectations in relation to how you interact with them in your role.

Effective relationships

Effective relationships occur if there is a fair balance between self-disclosure and feedback. As we self-disclose, we become more open with others regarding what we know about ourselves to be true (the façade is dropped). As we gain feedback from others perceiving us, we begin to see ourselves as others do (the blind spot is revealed to us).

Often by enlarging both these areas of self-disclosure and feedback we can extend our working with others into the unknown without fear of humiliation or rejection. In this way, each person is represented by his or her own window on the world.

Active listening skills are helpful to seek feedback from others and to increase self-knowledge. On the other hand, we all have defences protecting the parts of ourselves that we feel to be most vulnerable.

Probing the blind spot in team-building

Remember that the blind spot contains behaviour, feelings and motivations not accessible to the person, but which others can see at times or which emerge under pressure. Feelings of inadequacy, incompetence, impotence, unworthiness, rejection, guilt, dependency, ambivalence for loved ones, needs to control and to manipulate, are all difficult to face, and yet can be seen by others.

A word of caution in using techniques in team-building to probe the blind spot – to reveal forcibly what another wishes you not to see, can be seen as 'psychological rape', and can be traumatic. Fortunately, nature has provided us with a variety of defence mechanisms to cope with such events, such as denial, ignoring, rationalising, and other means of cushioning emotional pain.

On the simplest level, difficulties may arise due to a lack of clarity in the interaction, such as poor grammar or choice of words, unorganised thoughts, faulty logic, etc. This induces the receiver to criticise you, the sender, by revealing something that was in your blind quadrant. Then, if the feedback works, you correct it immediately, or if you are taking a more long-term view, take a course in reading and writing.

On a deeper level, you may be in a group meeting, and while you secretly sympathise with the minority viewpoint, you voted with the majority. However, blind to you, you actually may be communicating this information via body language, in conflict with your verbal message.

On an even deeper level, in an interaction with others you may always put on a smiling, happy face, hiding all negative feelings. By withholding negative feelings, you may be signalling to your friends to withhold also and to keep their distance. Thus, your communication style may seem bland or distant.

Inter-group relations

Leaders also have a big responsibility to promote a culture and expectation for open, honest, positive, helpful, constructive, sensitive communications, and the sharing of knowledge throughout their organisation.

Established team members logically tend to be more open than new team members. New team members have to learn to trust the others before much is shared by seeking and actively listening to feedback from other group members, given sensitively of course.

Thus new individuals build the confidence to disclose information or feelings about themselves to the group and group members. Managers and team leaders can play an important role in facilitating feedback and disclosure among group members, and in directly giving feedback to individuals about their own blind spot.

We all know how difficult it is to work well when kept in the dark. No one works well when subject to 'mushroom management'. People who are 'thick-skinned' tend to have a large 'blind spot'. By seeking or soliciting feedback from others, the aim should be to reduce this area and thereby to increase self-awareness. This blind area is not an effective or productive space for individuals or groups to remain in modern organisations.

This blind spot could also be referred to as ignorance about oneself, or issues in which one is deluded. A blind spot could also include issues that others are deliberately withholding from a person.

Managers should promote a climate of non-judgemental feedback, and group response to individual disclosure. This reduces fear and therefore encourages both processes to happen. However, remember the extent to which an individual seeks feedback must always be at the individual's own discretion. Some people are more resilient than others – care needs to be taken to avoid causing serious emotional upset.

Our 'hidden area'

We all have self-knowledge that is kept hidden from others. The hidden area could include sensitivities, fears, hidden agendas, manipulative intentions and secrets – anything that a person knows but does not reveal, for whatever reason. It's natural for very personal and private information and feelings to remain hidden, indeed, certain information, feelings and experiences have no bearing on work, and so can and should remain hidden. However, typically, a lot of hidden information is work, or performance-related and so is better revealed to the team.

Relevant hidden information and feelings enable better understanding, co-operation, trust, team-working effectiveness and productivity. Reducing hidden areas also minimises the potential for confusion, misunderstanding, poor communication, which all distract from and undermine team effectiveness.

Organisational culture and working atmosphere have a major influence on group members' preparedness to disclose their hidden selves. Most people fear judgement or vulnerability and therefore hold back hidden information and feelings. However, if revealed it would enhance mutual understanding and improve awareness, enabling better individual performance and group effectiveness.

The extent to which an individual discloses personal feelings and information, and the issues which are disclosed, and to whom, must always be at the individual's own discretion. Some people are more keen and able than others to disclose. People should disclose at a pace and depth that they find personally comfortable. As with feedback, some people are more resilient than others – care needs to be taken to avoid causing emotional upset.

Group discovery

There is a high degree of untapped potential in most employees. With the right climate for learning at work this can be explored as a group. New aptitudes can be quite close to the surface, and given some daylight without criticism can be positive and useful, or they can be deeper aspects of a person's personality, influencing their behaviour to various degrees. Subconscious behaviour and motivation would typically be expected in younger people, and people who lack experience or self-belief. These might include:

- an ability that is under-estimated or untried through lack of opportunity, encouragement, confidence or training
- a natural ability or aptitude that a person doesn't realise they possess or that has been inappropriately suppressed in later life
- a fear or aversion that a person does not know they have
- repressed subconscious feelings
- conditioned behaviour or attitudes from childhood (e.g. it is wrong for girls to seek praise).

The processes by which this information and knowledge can be uncovered are various:

- through self-discovery or observation by others
- through collective or mutual discovery
- through discovery experienced on outward bound courses
- through other deep or intensive group work.

Counselling can also uncover unknown issues, but this would then be known to the person and by one other, rather than by a group. The unknown area could also include repressed or subconscious feelings rooted in formative events and traumatic past experiences, which can stay unknown for a lifetime and in this context should not be used to address issues of a clinical nature.

A team that understands itself – that is, each person having a strong mutual understanding with the team – is far more effective than a team in which individual members do not relate to the team. Team members and leaders should always be striving to increase openness, and to reduce their blind spot, hidden and unknown areas.

Bruce Tuckman's 'Forming, Storming, Norming, Performing' team development model also relates to Emotional Intelligence theory, and one's awareness and development of Emotional Intelligence. In addition, but to a lesser but nonetheless interesting extent, this relates to the Hersey-Blanchard Situational Leadership team development and management styles model and also to Transactional Analysis.

The common principle is that as the team matures and communications improve, so performance improves too, as less energy is spent on clearing up in hindsight on internal issues and clarifying understanding, and more effort is devoted to external aims and productive output.

What relevance does EI have to me?

The start of self-awareness is to test your readiness to change. Are you motivated to change? Developing your EQ will help if you are concerned with:

- your influencing skills – wanting to understand others more in terms of what persuades them, what they can actively listen to and really hear
- stressful situations which get on top of you, cause you anxiety hours after they have occurred, or are woken in the night by them
- getting the message across to people unambiguously and being able to listen to them without inner dialogue disrupting your concentration
- your life/work balance because it must become more equitable and you need to renegotiate how your time is spent
- relationships that are stressful or even mystifying in terms of your behaviour or the reactions of others
- your general health being below what is accepted as a healthy norm and suspecting that it is self-inflicted injury in the form of bad habits, self-deprecation and lack of commitment.

Note any conclusions you reach about why EI is of interest or of use to you from the above list and your own ideas. Expect more conclusions to occur to you. Plan your next step for raising your EI competencies using this feedback.

The APET model

A psychological model of behaviour to complete our exploration of how emotions affect us is called the APET model. Studying it will deepen our understanding of why we behave the way we do. This is important and at the very core of developing our EI. When we have a full grasp of why we behave the way we behave, we can then move on to develop consistently productive and rewarding behaviour.

The APET model acknowledges the order in which we now know the different stages of perception and evaluation actually happen. It has implications for any other model that claims to be effective in changing behaviour. By this being understood, communication in business and in everyday life can be improved.

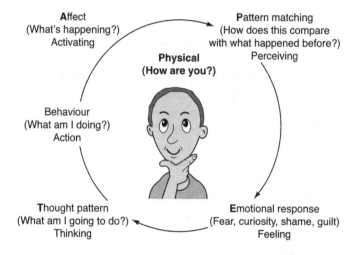

Figure 5.1: The APET model

A is the activating event
P is the pattern detection and matching process
E is the primary and secondary emotional response this gives rise to e.g. anger overlaying sadness
T is the thought pattern (if any) triggered by this response
(APET Model by Joe Griffin and Ivan Tyrell)

The primitive part of the brain known as the limbic system – the 'emotional brain' – assesses all incoming stimuli for potential threat before the conscious brain – the neocortex – is even aware of them. Where a threat is perceived, the limbic system triggers the 'fight or flight' reflex before the neocortex has even become aware of the 'threat', let alone had a chance to assess it.

If emotional arousal is sufficiently strong, it overrides the thinking brain altogether. Emotions operate from a good/bad, either/or perspective. 'High emotional arousal makes us stupid.'

Some implications of the APET model are:

- Communication with someone in a state of high emotional arousal is impossible. Only when a person is calm can their neocortex employ the subtle 'shades of grey' thinking and reframing abilities that allow adaptation of patterns and solving of problems. A calm state of mind is an essential precondition for cognitive interventions to work.
- Some traumatic events never make it to the neocortex to be verbalised and rationalised. Any recall of the traumatic event simply triggers the emotional response again. So, counselling for Post-Traumatic Stress Disorder (PTSD) which encourages the person to relive or 'talk through' the incident may well make the problem worse.
- In cases of depression, analytic or person-centred interventions, which encourage us to focus on and 'understand' the events of our lives, will tend to trigger emotional arousal and reinforce existing negative patterns. Metaphors and storytelling can be effective interventions for such problems because they engage our pattern-matching abilities without triggering emotional arousal, allowing them to find their own solutions.

While the discoveries underlying this model will be familiar to anyone taking a serious interest in current brain research, the APET is a simple and powerful model from which all other approaches to behaviour change can learn.

The applications don't stop there. In business, for example, any approach to organisational change which fails to manage the potential fear, uncertainty and doubt caused by inadequate communication is bound for a very rocky ride. This is particularly true in situations where multiple mergers have taken place over time and a pattern has emerged for the way this is handled. Once that fear has set in, it makes communication much more difficult, as any signals emanating from management are viewed with suspicion.

Taking control of your behavioural patterns

We can entrain ourselves to react differently, to react positively, and to use foresight rather than hindsight to manage our emotions. To be successful in this, we need to rehearse acquiring foresight frequently so that we become unconsciously competent in it. At this point we react in a different manner without really thinking about it. Just like switching on the lights on our new car without fumbling.

If you want to change a situation of never or rarely being able to manage unhelpful emotions or impulses you are going to have to:

- understand the cost to you of the related anxiety and stress and decide that you do not want to pay this price any longer
- understand the triggers that are unique to you as an individual
- commit to more reflection on your behaviour. Initially, this will be with hindsight but with practice you will catch yourself in the middle.

Eventually you will achieve foresight about unhelpful impulses and bad habits before you act on them. However, foresight must be backed with increasing self-discipline for you to halt and allow yourself to regain control. You must use the intervention of foresight to force yourself to a positive solution. Brain chemistry altered by anger takes 15 minutes to leave the system. Negative emotions coupled with a higher state of arousal cause more cortisol to be secreted which in the long term has serious health repercussions. More positive emotion opens up brain function and you find more ideas come to you.

You will also need to practise deconstructing the emotional roots of your behaviour in routine work situations. The effectiveness of meetings and their impact on stress levels is mainly due to human relationships. Before your next work meeting, look at the agenda as early as possible. Routine meetings have packed agendas. However, you can still raise your self-awareness and self-control using it as a vehicle. Find out how other attendees regard agenda items in advance. You can explain that you are doing self-development to make meetings more valuable.

INSTANT TIP

By improving interpersonal and relationship skills, staff will generate additional energy and vitality that is useful under pressure.

What benefits do my customers get?

The Marshmallow Test

Walter Mischel, an American academic and psychologist specialising in personality theory and social psychology, conducted a fascinating experiment with young children, which proved to be a predictor by the age of four of social intelligence in later life. The child was offered a single marshmallow immediately or two marshmallows if they could leave it alone while he went away for twenty minutes. Those who were able to resist temptation to eat the single marshmallow immediately showed higher social adaptability, as well as greater academic success than the rapid scoffers. Their ability to regulate their emotional responses was the foundation stone for behaving in an emotionally intelligent way in adulthood.

Thinking back to your childhood, were you one of those children who found it difficult to defer immediate gratification? How do you think your customer-facing staff would fare in this? Whatever the result, the good news is that EI is far more amenable to improvement in later life than IQ.

Strategic context for excellent service

If you asked yourself, 'What is our Service Strategy?', how would you grade yourself against the following criteria:

- **reliability**: the ability to perform the promised service dependably and accurately
- **assurance**: the knowledge and courtesy of employees and their ability to convey trust and confidence
- **tangibles**: the appearance of physical facilities, equipment, personnel and communication materials
- **empathy**: the provision of caring, individualised attention to each customer
- **responsiveness**: the willingness to help customers and provide prompt service.

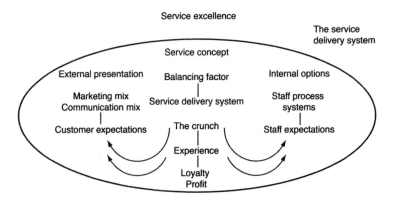

Figure 6.1: Service strategy

Would you be able to answer the following based on your knowledge of current operations? Would any of your staff know the answers too?

- How well is your organisation rated externally?
- What is the marketing mix and messages?
- What are your customer expectations?
- How is this met or exceeded by your staff?
- What is the customer experience?

Do current campaign management practices put the customer at the heart of what you do? This is part of being an emotionally intelligent organisation where everything stems from the premise that the customer is at the core.

The service triangle

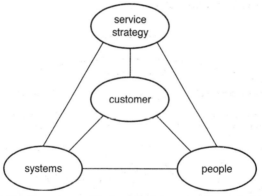

Figure 6.2: Putting the customer at the heart of what you do – the service triangle

In their 'service triangle' (see Figure 6.2) Albrecht and Zemke identified a number of characteristics that could be identified in all the organisations recognised as providers of excellent customer service. In all these organisations, the customer was central to everything they did. The foundation of a successful service operation is a well-defined service strategy that directs the attention of the people in the organisation to the real priorities of its customers. The strategy should be a non-trivial statement of intent, must make a noticeable difference and must be deliverable. The service strategy should be uppermost in the mind of all the staff in the organisation and all the activities in the organisation should be directed to fulfilling the strategy.

The systems by which the products and services of the company are delivered to the customer must be designed for the convenience of the customers but at the same time should be easy to use for the employees. They should be self-correcting and invisible to the customer.

The people who are in direct contact with the customer are the most visible part of the model. They must be responsive, attentive and willing to help the customer in any way. They should be empowered to work on behalf of the customers and the function of all those who are not in direct contact with the customers should be to support them. This means high levels of Emotional Intelligence in the way they interact internally and externally. This requires excellent practices amongst supervisors for team learning so that the bar is raised as part of everyday learning at work. For example, asking regularly:

1. What was your most powerful learning experience?
   - What was happening that made it powerful for me?
   - What did I do that made it powerful?
   - What did others do?
   - How do other peak learning experiences compare?
2. Reflecting on experience and learning – what is the core essence at work?
3. What are your hopes and wishes for the future?

Moments of truth

Jan Carlzon, the president of SAS, first articulated the concept of 'Moments of Truth', in his book of the same name. SAS used the

'Moments of Truths' concept, together with a particular targeting of the business traveller market, as the basis of their business strategy in the early 1980s at the time of the oil crisis. In the first year of utilising the strategy the company was able to increase earnings by $80m at a time when the combined losses of other airlines were in excess of $2bn. In the first three years of the strategy SAS was able to increase the number of full fare passengers by 23 per cent and discount passengers by 7 per cent in a stagnant market.

A moment of truth is any particular point of time where the customer interacts with the products, systems, people or procedures of an organisation, and makes a judgement about the quality of the organisation itself or the products and services it provides.

Each moment of truth provides an opportunity to delight the customer and reinforce his or her perception of the organisation as one that they like to do business with. Conversely, each one provides a potential point of dissatisfaction with the product or service received with the ultimate result that the customer might be lost.

The 'Moments of Truth' concept requires a particular organisational structure whereby the frontline employees, who interact with the customer, are empowered to take whatever steps are necessary to ensure customer satisfaction in line with the overall goals and strategy of the organisation. The role of management in such a system is to support and facilitate the frontline staff in performing this role. Carlzon describes this structure as a flattening of the traditional pyramid of the organisation. He says:

> 'Any business organisation seeking to establish a customer orientation and create a good impression during its 'moments of truth' must flatten the pyramid – that is, eliminate the hierarchical ties of responsibility in order to respond quickly and directly to customers' needs. The customer-oriented company is organised for change.'
>
> Jan Carlzon, *Moments of Truth*, Harper Business, 1987

EI for service success

When the service is provided by human contact, whether it is face-to-face, over the phone or a messaging system, the quality of interaction with the customer is driven by the Emotional Intelligence of both parties – you as the supplier and the customer's ability to interact and express their needs and wants. The factors which influence the provisions and perceptions of service quality at each stage of the process are summarised in the following diagrams. These are the moments when customers decide to go elsewhere or to stay with you and even recommend your service to others (known as advocacy):

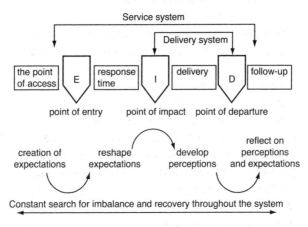

Figure 6.3: The customer processing model

At the point of access, depending on the handling by your staff, the customer starts a decision-making process, choosing between your own and competing service providers. The criteria will be:

- understanding of the customer processing operation
- ability to balance customer and staff expectations
- identifiable range of achievable expectations
- identified market segment.

This is where the investment in developing your staff pays off in acquiring, satisfying and creating referrals to new customers. Each of the following steps involves 20 per cent process training and 80 per cent rapport and relationship-forming guiding the customer through to the end transaction.

- **A point of access**: the customer's first moment of awareness of your existence is raised through advertising or other means and this creates expectations of the service they would receive.
- **E (Point of entry)**: the customer's first interaction with the service (in person or by phone, fax, email etc.) is where the first expectations would be reshaped positively or negatively.
- **Response time**: the time the customer is waiting for a response and develops perceptions of good or bad service.
- **I (Point of impact)**: initial acknowledgement of and response to the customer in the service system. Here the customer continues to develop expectations and perceptions of good or bad service. This depends on the skill level of members of staff in rapport, leading and pacing customers through needs and options for products and services.
- **Delivery**: provision of the service and associated products to the customer:
  - staff ability to recognise requirements, negotiate treatment and personalise service
  - staff social skills.
- **D (Point of departure)**: the customer physically leaves the service system. Customers begin to reflect on expectations and perceptions of good or bad service. This is related to the ability of staff to:
  - assess mismatches
  - assess customer concerns

 - show recognition of the customer view
 - negotiate appropriate recovery and appease if
   necessary.
- **Follow-up**: reflection by the customer on the quality of
  the service they have received and on the appropriate
  action taken on redressing mismatches.

What is vital is identifying the discriminating competencies that satisfy customers and convert them to advocates of your business. This needs to follow the flow of the customer as illustrated and performance needs to be picked up at these points. This is why team managers must have the sensitivities associated with high degrees of social awareness in order to observe their team members and communicate feedback effectively.

A Tier 1 service provider completed a £6 million pound study to investigate the business model for a new Internet bank launch project. This produced a number of criteria used in the design of the brand and the competencies needed by employees to deliver the business model. For example:

- it is in low EQ moments that we may lose a good
  employee, sale or a client
- it is 16 times harder to win back a client than to win new
  business
- a dissatisfied client will tell 15 people
- an advocate (very satisfied) will tell five people that your
  service or product is invaluable to them; you gain these
  clients at very low cost
- therefore, three times as many people are told about your
  product or service through dissatisfaction than the
  opposite, so the economics are clear.

In order to convert all customers to advocate your business to others, how do you ensure that they perceive they are getting the GOLD standard of service (linked to what each customer is worth to you)? How do you manage client energy levels around what you offer, when this year's USP (Unique Selling Point) is perceived by them as next year's ordinary service level (as illustrated)?

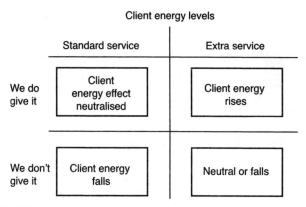

Figure 6.4: Client service levels – the energy and enthusiasm that clients have wane as last year's extra service becomes this year's standard expectation

This is all part of your service strategy and justifies why staff need regular training and development at being 'in the shoes of the customer' and feeding back on operational experience. In the next section, we look at specific EI competencies more generically in selling.

EI for sales success

Emotional competencies are fundamental in selling, along with the particular competencies of optimism and recovering from setback. The salesperson that knows the product inside out will not succeed without the additional ability to forge strong relationships. To do so the salesperson must win trust, be accurate in their emotional awareness of the client and cope with their own feelings, such as disappointment.

There is plenty of anecdotal evidence that high Emotional Intelligence helps to make sales. People buy from people. If you get on well with customers, they are more likely to buy. There is sound research evidence as well.

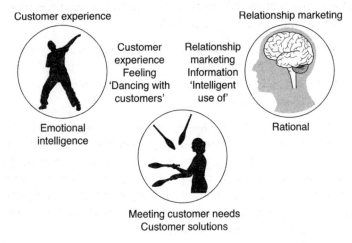

Figure 6.5: The customer processing model is a constant search for imbalance and ways to recover balance in customer transactions

Standing in the shoes of the customer

Empathy is another EI competency that is fundamental. Marketing people work in abstract subtleties: 'What is the hint of a perception of a customer need?' Understanding how the client feels and what is important to them gives vital information.

Salespeople work on a more tangible level: 'Does this person want the product at all? If not, it is better to look elsewhere. If they do, do they want this particular brand? What could be done to make it more advantageous?' The salesperson who starts at customer needs, then looks for ways to accommodate those needs, is more likely to sell than one who starts with the product, and attempts to mould the customer to fit it.

Empathy is also a factor in rapidly building trusting relationships. Trust is particularly important in sales, as it is becoming more and more difficult to differentiate between products in a particular sector for any length of time. This means that the quality of the relationship with the salesperson can make the difference between a sale and a loss.

- How accountable do ordinary members of staff feel for winning more business?
- How is individual competence linked to customer follow-through business?

Customers experience the degree of care they want when their account managers are emotionally intelligent; the account manager picks up on the needs of the customer quickly and easily. They know when they want a quick exchange and when they want to chat for a while. They are able skilfully to diffuse a complaint because they have built up such rapport and trust with the customer and know what influences them.

You will recognise that society is growing more and more diverse. Salespeople are likely to meet customers from a wide range of socio-economic groups, nationalities or religions and need to form good relationships with them. This means being sensitive to different viewpoints, being able to challenge your own assumptions when confronted by a distinction. As well as deductive reasoning, this takes high self-esteem, self-awareness and empathy, all of which are emotional competencies.

- Do you know all the stages that your customers go through whilst being handled by operations?
- Do you know the economics involved in advocates, dissatisfied customers and every option in-between?
- How accountable do ordinary members of staff feel for the state changes that customers go through?
- How is individual competence linked to customer satisfaction?

Are you a glass half-empty or a glass half-full person?

Optimism is also an EI competence needed by salespeople. Selling can be gruelling; you need resilience too. Selling can involve disappointment when there is a lot at stake; you will rarely control all of the factors facing the buying behaviour and dominant buying motive of the customer. Those who sink quickly into despair when matters outside their control adversely impact a sale may become casualties of the pressure. Martin Seligman, psychology professor at the University of Pennsylvania, and pioneer of the field of positive psychology, measured insurance salespeople in terms of learned optimism. This showed increased sales to the tune of 37 per cent.

As just one example, L'Oreal changed its salespersons' recruitment policy to allow for the emotional competencies of the applicants. The result was a dramatic increase in sales and a corresponding reduction in turnover of staff.

Self-motivation is a self-fuelling sales reward system. Those who have the inner will to succeed, persevere. They own their performance and monitor it themselves. They find ways to improve: 'If it isn't broke, look again.'

Those salespeople whose self-motivation pivots around incentives are unlikely to succeed in the long term. It is a job that requires drive – and determination to achieve, with accurate self-assessment and the resilience to recover from disappointments:

- How do staff allow for and cope with the varying maturity and experience of the client in campaign management?
- How is individual competence linked to their success at targeting varying scales of organisation or industry type?

Superior sales performers

Some organisations believe that the research is overwhelming: the critical differentiators for a superior versus average sales force are EI-based. Superior sales performers:

- sense others' development needs and bolster their abilities
- cultivate opportunities through diverse people
- read the political and social currents in an organisation
- anticipate, recognise, meet and exceed customer needs
- understand customers' needs and match them to services or products
- seek ways to increase customers' satisfaction and loyalty
- gladly offer appropriate assistance
- grasp a customer's perspective, acting as a trusted adviser
- sense others' feelings, perspectives and take an active interest in their concerns
- are attentive to emotional cues and listen well
- are sensitive to and understanding of others' perspectives
- assist by understanding other people's needs and feelings
- listen openly and empathetically, sending convincing responses
- are effective in give-and-take, registering emotional cues to attune their message
- deal with difficult issues in a straightforward manner
- are seeking of mutual understanding and welcoming of full disclosure
- foster open communication, coping with the adverse as much as the beneficial news.

Globalisation is driving teams to have transcultural competencies as well as the localised capabilities to deal with the demographics of their sales regions. Given the opportunity to work with a discrete sales group in order to demonstrate the impact of EI techniques, we know improvements will be seen and measured in total sales, win–loss ratio improvements and deal profitability.

Sales teams need self-awareness, self-control and awareness of others. Most professionals need to be adept at both interpreting the emotional roots to their thinking and behaviour and *choosing* actions to influence outcomes. It is essential for salespeople to be capable of making good insights into the behaviour of others, to be consistently successful and to sustain profitable relationships with customers.

As with IQ, everyone has a starting basis across the EQ scale, but EQ can be developed throughout life. Emotional learning involves changing habits such as:

- learning to approach people positively rather than avoiding them when a sales relationship is at risk
- listening actively to clients – not only being silent as a pause before you speak, but actively listening with empathic communication designed to first gain understanding of the client or prospect before seeking to transmit a sales message
- giving feedback skilfully, for example, if you need a client to understand why a project did not go as planned due to a failure on their side of the customer/supplier interface.

Sales teams need stamina and resilience. Sales team performance is undermined by poorly addressed 'human factors'. For example, every day an estimated 270,000 people in the UK across all industries take time off work because of work-related stress: this represents a cumulative cost in terms of sick pay, lost production and NHS charges of around £7 billion annually. In a survey of 600 workers, one third thought about quitting their jobs and 14 per cent actually did (from 'Pressure Points – a survey into the causes and consequences of occupational stress in UK academic and related staff' by Gail Kinman, Association of University Teachers). A Chartered Management Institute survey indicated that over 80 per cent of the 1,100 managers who responded experienced symptoms of stress such as tiredness, irritability and disturbed sleep.

The most professional companies have been highly successful at creating 'A' category sales forces. However, the demands and challenges of today's pressurised market mean that energy, enthusiasm and the ability to feel powerful in negotiations is being undermined and depleted. This is resulting in an inability to achieve sales goals.

It is now accepted that this disabling of performance is due to work pressure and workplace stress. When the 'A' team sales force is falling by the wayside, it is clearly time to act.

Salespeople are in the communications business, as are many roles today – whether the job title is sales manager, business analyst, journalist, caterer etc. Authentic communication means that your words and actions are aligned and the intended message is received and understood. If there is a gap between what was intended and what was interpreted then the resulting outcome will not meet expectations. It is vital that salespeople are excellent communicators.

What is the range of possible interventions?

Cognitive skills are called 'hard' skills, while those associated with Emotional Intelligence are called 'soft'. There are some hard costs to poor soft skills. It is at the very moment that unproductive behaviour is triggered that we may lose a sale or worse, a client. Only through understanding what occasionally triggers unproductive behaviour (low EQ) can we determine self-knowledge as a basis for change.

It is estimated that 70 per cent of the reasons customers leave is down to low EQ – are you investing the majority of your development funds in the wrong area?

Cognitive skills have traditionally been given a higher value than emotional competencies. Is this justified in terms of return on investment? It would be worth completing an analysis of why customers have been lost or sales lost by subdividing the reasons given into EQ-related reasons (the human side of doing business) and the more technical, process or product design-related aspects.

Other studies have compared different EI competencies and the significance of them on different professional sales groups. Sales directors may be interested in a study to identify discriminating competencies for their particular business to spread excellent performance around the team. This will help refine recruitment and selection, induction and development of staff.

Improving the experience you give your customers

As illustrated in the customer process model earlier (see Figure 6.3) the experience is generated in real time, managed and brought to a close. To create improvements you would:

- design an explorative and creative process with exercises involving all parties
- use Emotional Intelligence competencies to generate sustainable, profitable relationships with customers and optimise internal working relationships
- utilise techniques to elicit each individual's success story

and apply this to circumstances challenging the customer-facing team so that we move away from the language of human deficit

- combine systems, processes, behavioural and product competencies with values and attitudes where harmony in the whole is far greater than the sum of the parts
- design the techniques for dialogue and activities between sales agents and the customer through whatever media (face-to-face, telephone, email, messaging, etc.). All practical interactions in each medium need to be created to complete the Customer Experience, for example:
  - greetings and salutations
  - handling people in difficulties
  - acquiring personal information
  - placing and servicing orders
  - handling special projects
  - ensuring customers come back with an order when they need time to think
  - transferring customers seamlessly around the company.

One of the most powerful exercises in creating a distinction (the Customer Experience) is the result of experiencing a number of other competitor services. Deconstruction of these experiences will lead to deeper insight into the true customer interaction. This is a systemic approach which can lead to breakthroughs in learning which will be used in design of the *ultimate Customer Experience*. This information is essentially tacit knowledge – things you did not know you knew until asked a question or put in a situation demanding a solution.

You need to use sound psychology-based approaches for training and development purposes. The focus may rest on:

- Making best use of existing Emotional Intelligence competencies to allow staff to be self-aware, to be self-regulating even in difficult circumstances and to have great socio-cultural skills intuitively and in rapport with the client. This is not only to generate sustainable, profitable relationships with customers but also to optimise working relationships.

● Eliciting each individual's success story and applying this to circumstances challenging the customer-facing team. (For example, using techniques to facilitate systemic learning in individuals and the team.) This gets away from the language of human deficit prevalent in some workplaces and actually engages the brain in a different and more generative fashion.

● The combination of systems, process, behavioural and product competencies with values and attitudes where harmony in the whole is far greater than the sum of the parts.

● Creating the competence for important distinctions defined by you.

In essence, creating accredited sales personnel where the quality of the customer experience meets and exceeds expectations.

Campaign planning, closure and review checklist

It is essential to review the hard processes and the soft skills aspects at the end of each campaign, particularly where it leads to success. This learning can then be disseminated evenly and appropriately across the organisation.

● How do staff allow for the varying maturity and experience of the client in campaign management?

- How is individual competence linked to targeting the customer for varying scales of organisation or industry type?
- How is objectivity got into the system? It is important to set realistic campaign objectives and have a review of campaigns upon completion.
- End of campaign reports (remember – **honesty pays**).
  - internally (in terms of what went wrong, what went right)
  - externally (in terms of this is what we got, but here are the improvements we think we could make on the next campaign and why, etc.).
- What is a customer worth?
  - What is the yield per campaign?
  - How are cross-sales or opportunities to upsell identified?
  - Are there fees for leads to suppliers of complementary services?
- How do staff achieve objectivity in the company system?
  - internally (in terms of what went wrong, what went right)
  - externally (in terms of this is what we got and lessons learned or improvements).
- How is individual competence measured in the performance appraisal?
- How is the feedback communicated?
- Consider if your customers feel:
  - respected
  - important
  - remembered
  - acknowledged
  - satisfied
  - helped
  - understood.

Customer service

1. Teach representatives to look for and validate feelings.
2. Ask what would help the customer feel better.
3. Set goals for key customer feelings.
4. Track them and manage them.
5. Use a simple scale such as 0–10 for each feeling.
6. Avoid saying things like:
   - 'It is company policy.'
   - 'I am not authorised to do that.'
   - 'There is nothing I can do.'
   - 'You should have got the person's name.'

INSTANT TIP

What benefits do my customers get? Better service! Investing the majority of your development funds in cognitive skills ignores research that 70 per cent of the customers leave due to low EQ in your staff.

07

How does EI accelerate management of change?

Managing change requires all the classic activities such as planning, organising, allocating resources, monitoring and control. This chapter addresses these hard management skills in the context of a change programme whilst also inviting the reader to look deeper at the use of Emotional Intelligence in making leadership more successful and in providing employees with the wherewithal to leave the past behind and engage with change.

Developing change organisational roles

Recent research (2003) by the DTI and DfES revealed that the UK is falling behind in the international business performance league tables. The research lays the blame squarely with management skills and leadership. Recognising that the UK has a long and proud history of business excellence, the global marketplace now means that we need to do what we do even better.

Traditional leadership no longer meets people's expectations. We need to understand:

● the utility of leadership with Emotional Intelligence (which is pervasive as discussed later in the chapter)
● what it is in inspirational leaders that makes people want to follow them
● how these leaders impact their organisations through their people.

A change programme where roles are clearly understood and effectively undertaken is much more likely to succeed and to be sustained into the long term. There are five distinct stakeholder roles in any change project. Three of these work much more closely together routinely: the change leader, the change agent and the change target.

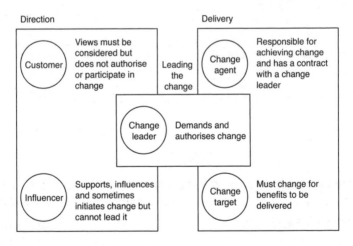

Figure 7.1: Change network

Individuals can fulfil more than one role, especially as the change programme progresses. Customers and other influencers will be kept in the loop by means of a communications plan and targeted actions.

The role of the change leader is especially critical. The change leader has the biggest impact on the organisation, so poor change leadership almost guarantees failure. Most leaders have something to learn about becoming effective leaders of change usually in terms of Emotional Intelligence rather than project or programme leadership.

We can define change leadership as:

'Behaving in a way that clearly demonstrates personal commitment and resolve for the people aspects of strategic change at every stage of its implementation'.

All parties involved in the effective management of change need to:

- recognise that they have a legitimate personal stake in the outcomes
- actively demonstrate personal change and its impact
- be realistic about the benefits to individuals and the emotional costs of change
- engage and enrol others – in the leadership team and elsewhere in the organisation.

If there are gaps in any of these, the change effort will suffer and you may need to consider a more comprehensive leadership development programme.

Developing a change agenda

The change wheel illustrated (see Figure 7.2) identifies a whole series of activities related to each other in several themes:

- top management leadership behaviours
- knowledge sharing
- trusting relationships as an effective interface
- clarity of purpose and communication.

Most of the items require high Emotional Intelligence in their application:

- **Top leadership** – being a good role model; dealing with myths having a negative impact; being sensitive to the attachments staff have to the previous culture's symbols and artefacts.
- **Clarity of purpose and communication** – the skill to craft the message to engender attitudinal changes; changes in understanding of the way things are done; behavioural changes to match a new culture.
- **Knowledge sharing** – when individuals feel insecure as they do going through change, leaders need to develop a deep resolve to lead through it. They might need coaching skills much of which are awareness-based; they need excellent networking skills and they must be skilled at utilising multiple channels and media to expand knowledge sharing.
- **Effective interface (trusting relationships)** – 50 per cent of time at work is wasted through lack of trust where people are clearing up issues or dwelling on them rather than being productive. Leaders need to form strong psychological contracts with people; they need excellent communication competence and they must understand how to allow dialogue for the impacts of change to emerge and not be buried.

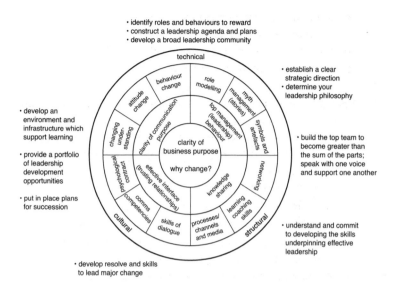

Figure 7.2: The change wheel

Wider development programme

The detail of this development requirement could fill a book in itself but, typically, the following need to be part of the training programme for those in the change organisation:

- **Leadership styles** – consciously having more than one style, adapting to get better results.
- **Being** – self-awareness and self-regulation especially dealing with colleagues under pressure. Social awareness, influencing and the ability to develop others (transitioning the through-change impacts).
- **Doing** – understanding impact of changes personally and being a role model for change: 'Fit for Change'.

- **Having** – getting a grip on own development needs, in terms of predicting skills, know-how and development needs: 'Headroom for growth'.

The change organisation directs the change programme through to its conclusion until everyone intended to be in the new organisation has completed the intended employee development process.

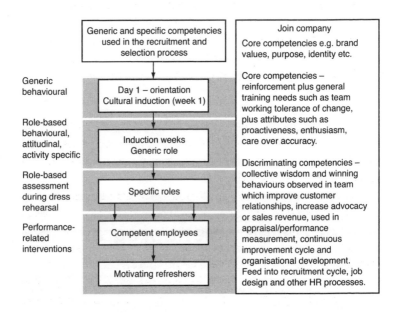

Figure 7.3: Employee development lifecycle

Change targets usually buy into this process of employee development because they can see what is in it for them. They are clear about where they are going and who they want to be in the changed organisation.

Change plan and the critical path for implementation

At each stage the change organisation needs good management information on:

- likely emotional responses to the intended change
- what is involved in the implementation
- what messages have been disseminated and to whom
- external sources of communication and any which are affecting reputation and the ability to continue the programme.

There is a need for everyone in the initial change organisation to absorb the plan and conduct a 'brown paper and sticky note' exercise to think through each function's own complementary strategy, HR, IT, production, etc.

You might want to run some of the top team-building events first which generate a Change Management Plan as highlighted in the Change Wheel diagram (see Figure 7.2). The wisdom behind this is that you may need to explore with them what the changes that you wish to make would feel like to them and let them see how it would impact on them. The apparent 'permission to change' is usually granted after 'permission to explore what this change feels like' is given, and those who do not recognise this get sabotaged.

You will effectively produce a critical path or optimal sequence for typically the next 18 months to two years and be able to create management milestones once you have the big picture. You can illustrate the dependency of one outcome on earlier initiatives and processes should anybody try to challenge your decisions.

Basic guidelines: Create the timeline across the top and bottom for the next two years. Work backwards. Fill in sticky notes with desired outcomes, potential threats and opportunities e.g. new competitors in market, new technology loses market share, share price hits x pounds (people take the money and run, etc.). Include all your ideas for activities, HR processes and use string, thin tape or a pen to create links. Stay high level and work out detail on separate sheets. You can take digital photographs or get it turned into some planning tool – project management or Visio, for example.

Change management or business process checklists

Most industries, commercial sectors and public sector departments have an accepted model of must-have processes with clear links between them that you may want to debate and sort out functional leaders. It is important to consider the management system when developing the organisation. This will help to distinguish what supports or impedes the development of the organisation.

Few change programmes have the resources to change the whole population of the workforce. Prioritisation has to take place to invest in those above the 'let it happen' line and recruit for missing skills and take them through the employee development process outlined earlier to 'create the vision'.

The options for programme strategy are reflected in Table 7.1.

		End result	
		Transformation	Realignment
Nature	Incremental	Evolution – 2	Adaptation – 1
	Big Bang	Revolution – 3	Reconstruction – 4

Table 7.1: Options for programme strategy

The options 1–4 can be described as:

Option 1: base case – adaptation. No transformation work is defined in this option. This may be a post-merger situation, where it is not in a steady state scenario. The organisation already has a stream of adaptive changes that realign sites and make incremental changes. Therefore it has no opportunity to evaluate the cost of 'doing nothing' as would traditionally be argued in the base case option for a change programme. There is no transformation agenda and the pace would be set locally.

Option 2: organic development from current organisation design – evolution. This option means that transformation will be completed as incremental changes alongside the operational work (small, non-urgent projects under line management). The overall plan would be a transformation in values, behaviours, processes, locations, structures, systems and staff. However, the focus would remain decentralised and prone to local interpretation within each site. There would be choices on how visible it became and the pace would be set centrally.

Option 3: big bang programme – revolution. The transformation is launched with high impact and fast pace. The resources dedicated to transformation and customers are consulted as to the knock-on effect on their demand falling within the 18-month major intervention. Control is more centralised and aligned to a single

Option 1 is achievable if customer's expectations are managed because demand still exceeds supply. Risk-averse organisations would be well rewarded for acknowledging this more tactical choice and implementing change solely on this basis. However, it may not be the choice for the organisation's own long-term survival. A competitive situation, may just not have surfaced yet.

Option 2 is achievable but not without assertive management of demand and good influencing strategies. The management strategy would be more in comfort zone for leaders and managers than Options 3 and 4. The latter require further leadership and management development. The programme management function would have to create more pull from the working level.

Option 3 achieves absolute clarity about the organisation of the future within six to eight months of launch and people become clear about how much of a stretch this is for them (do they change or go). It requires strong, consistent leadership and heightened toleration of uncertainty. Not for risk-averse managers. If committed to it would require significant resilience but could deliver outstanding results in a 15–18 month timeframe.

Option 4 is very strategic and communicative with significant potential savings by sharing and learning from others provided the mindset to do so is achieved. It is probably much easier to adopt this approach than it seems because of the coincidental way in which transformation has been developed thus far. More explanation and exploration would be required before an informed decision could be made to adopt or reject this option.

brand. The programme would be highly visible to all top management and the customer but with different communities participating at different stages.

Option 4: business strategy-driven – reconstruction. The organisation is realigned in a strategically driven initiative using a World Class framework such as the UK Business Excellence Model (UK BEM). This European framework, started in the 1970s was funded by BP, Shell, BT and others. It starts by developing the leadership and the change organisation as discussed earlier in the chapter.

This option becomes very public in its later stages, literally exposing the organisation's position within a global benchmark. The advantage is 25 years' worth of shared learning made available through Best Practice Clubs associated with the UK Business Excellence Model. The programme would be visible within the organisation through a communication plan with customer communities participating to different degrees. The focus would be on processes, policies and strategies across internal (the value chain) and the external customer boundaries (the demand chain). The entire supply chain to the business or as third parties to customers would be reviewed. Results are measured on customer, people and community satisfaction bases and there would be more choice on the pace set for change.

Challenging preconceived and limited views of learning

Effective ways of augmenting learning can be cross-functional teams and learning sets tackling real company issues in a programme of workshops, working groups and lectures by specialists.

Where change programmes are to an existing organisation and not building new ones, there will be potential friction points with exisiting policies and practice. These can be predicted and managed effectively. The change management organisation needs to assist HR in resolving the potential dilemma of evaluating development needs of individuals whilst they are being performance assessed relating to their pay. People often will not admit to change impacts and their need for development if they believe that such admission will count against them in their pay packet.

People behave as they are rewarded. Different people are drawn towards rewards, other people need to be motivated away (from fear, loss injury, etc.). In the last few years, tangible rewards may have been slow to change due to employment law, fear of litigation and the amount of consultation required with unions or individual bargaining.

Change approach

As you may know, any other approach than starting with the 'leaders modelling the new' will not work and may be sabotaged. First line supervisors in western societies have the most influence over change targets and their willingness to adopt changes. On a limited budget, the executive and first line supervision levels need to be brought together. Potential sabotage may stem from:

- slowing up within the middle management layers if any exist
- disruption from supervisors not selected for the change network
- resistance – strong individuals may be loud and destructive in disseminating their objections to change.

The executive presence during transition must be highly visible at working levels. Placing an HR partner in the change network is a potential countermeasure.

What is occurring is that people are going through the change curve illustrated in Figure 7.4. This is much the same as grief – grieving for the previous status quo of their role, job, colleagues, place of work and so on.

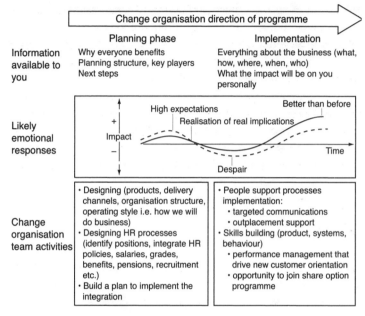

Figure 7.4: The change cycle

The change organisation has to ensure it has a comprehensive set of information being fed into it as well as anticipate and respond to the emotional response of the community (which may include strikes and media attention in some scenarios). Tables can be used to track progress with columns such as:

1. item number
2. change management critical success factors
3. main outcome, product or final action
4. dependent on action by...
5. timing.

The change approach for transformation covers four activity areas, namely:

1. **Foundation of education** – consistent development of core and discriminating competencies through the learning and development functions.
2. **Intervention** – the specific events run to drive change down through the change network and to augment two-way communication from top to bottom of the organisation.
3. **Participation** – this represents the necessary release of employees and managers to participate in education and change events.
4. **Communications** – a consistent, targeted and intelligent set of channels, media and methods designed to inform stakeholders and encourage them to complete the change programme.

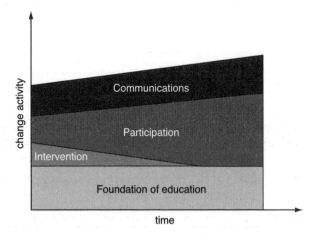

Figure 7.5: The change approach for transformation

Considering the number of events, the following method can be used to greatly improve the value of them called for by change programme activity. It encourages good chairmanship skills. For example, for every change product planned to be delivered, project managers are to take a '3D' approach to defining the activities associated with the delivery.

1. **TASK focus** – managing content, change goals and activities (this is the bit we are usually good at).
2. **PROCEDURES focus** – methods and techniques (this is the bit where we must consider methods and techniques suitable for organisational development). Having a timed agenda and sticking to it is one example.
3. **PROCESS focus** – interactions between people, feelings and emotions (this is the bit that is often not considered). This means the Chairperson intervenes and the participants are able to contribute evenly in discussion as appropriate to the agenda and their role at the meeting or specialism.

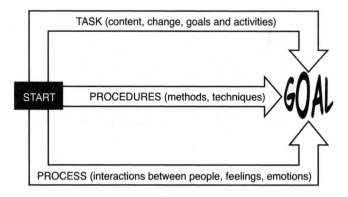

Figure 7.6: 3 Dimensions of managing change

Programme management controls

Management controls to be established will include:

- programme organisation (including roles and responsibilities)
- recruitment, selection and appointment
- reporting structure and cycle
- meetings required and structure.
- baseline plans.

Technical controls will contribute to specialist work being completed on time, within budget and to quality criteria. This will mean the selection of methods, practices and techniques appropriate for the content.

The programme Quality Management System will cover quality controls for 'right first time' production, 'fit for purpose' quality assurance and quality audit. Responsibility for quality control and quality assurance will rest with the technical streams. Quality audit will be conducted by the programme function.

INSTANT TIP

Arrange to meet someone highly regarded at work to exchange ideas about the change readiness of the organisation and discuss sharing these with senior management.

08

How does EI restore a work/life balance?

What is work/life balance?

People who believe they have equilibrium in their work/life balance are essentially saying they are not suffering undue stress. A work/life balance is a dynamic equilibrium, as no one's private life ever follows a monotonous pattern without peaks and troughs. How these are negotiated with work demands is where the skill lies. Enlightened employers offer employees choices designed to get what they need as an organisation but within flexible working arrangements to enrich the lifestyle of the employee. This tends to lead to staff remaining longer and being productive provided there is reasonable supervision and the right employee engagement.

Drawing on the emerging evidence from neuroscience, tackling stress issues means treating stress and emotion as if they were one. To treat them as separate fields is absurd. By recognising the interdependence between stress and emotions approaches are in essence enhancing an individual's EQ.

How well do you believe you balance your time between work and play, between family and employer? As often happens, if there are feelings that the balance is not right, some typical reasons may be:

- you enjoy work
- you fear jeopardising your career
- you perceive that your boss expects it
- you endure a workaholic organisational culture
- you think that you have to prove you can cope.

The nature of stress

The word stress is derived from the Latin word *stringere*, which means 'to draw tight'. According to Dr Lawrence E. Hinkle, Jr, Cornell University Medical College, New York (a medical doctor who has researched work and stress-related sudden deaths), 'in the seventeenth century the word was used to describe hardship or affliction'.

In the long term people react badly with either too little or too much stress. Without some sense of challenge (known as eustress, or 'good' stress, sensed as exhilaration and excitement) we would not get out of bed. In everyday situations, the stressful experience is pleasurable because one survives the threat.

Stress is an aspect of living that can be beneficial when it motivates, inspires or encourages change. Distress is when individuals perceive that they do not have the resources to cope with a perceived situation from the past, present or future.

One definition of stress is:

'A state that we experience when there is a mismatch between perceived demands and perceived ability to cope with the demands. It is the balance between how we view demands and how we think we can cope with those demands. This determines whether we feel no stress, distressed or what is known as eustressed.'

Professor T. Looker

The stress cycle

The fight or flight response has been well researched and monitored. It develops in the following cycle:

- The forebrain receives danger signals from eyes, ears, etc.
- The hypothalamus, in the brain, activates the pituitary gland to release hormones.
- Senses are activated, e.g. the pupils of the eyes dilate.
- Breathing rate increases and gets deeper. Heart rate and blood pressure increase.
- The liver releases sugar, cholesterol and fatty acids into the blood stream.
- Digestion ceases and bladder and bowel openings contract.
- The adrenal glands release hormones, adrenaline, noradrenaline and cortisol, which increase sweating and blood clotting ability.
- The most common symptom is that people don't feel well and medical practitioners can find no clinical reason.

Stress-related illness

Being constantly stressed causes illness because the metabolic change is continuous, preventing relaxation or proper sleep for the body and mind to repair itself. Some long-term effects can be: hair loss, headaches, migraines, strokes, impaired immune responses, nervousness, bad sleeping, neck and shoulder aches, lower back and leg aches, asthma, skin conditions, high blood pressure, bad circulation, heart diseases, some cancers, indigestion, ulcers, irritable bowel syndrome, impotency, menstrual disorders and rheumatoid arthritis. The negative effects of stress are also evident in the form of bad decision-making, negative internal politics, reduced creativity and apathy.

The coping mechanisms (alcohol, drugs, food, sex, dangerous sports, etc.) used to maintain a fast-paced lifestyle fuel illness eventually. The apparent ability to cope can lead to more upon more layers of stress-inducing situations being endured. This is often the most significant factor in illnesses that end careers. If optimum performance is continually maintained or surpassed (chronic stress), then performance deteriorates rapidly and people eventually become ill or die. Chronic stress is a cumulative phenomenon that can develop over a lifetime or over a few weeks. A vicious circle or rather spiral is entered into with the stress response to fear driving an individual to produce more effort for less performance, with more time spent working and less in relaxation.

Often it is not the obvious 'stress straw' that 'breaks the camel's back'. In the working environment, chronic stress often develops from a lifestyle encouraged by employers to gain short-term competitive advantage which is then compounded in the employee's life by an event such as a bereavement or house move. Absenteeism generated by chronic stress can cause a 'domino' collapse of employees as each person experiences overload when coping with their own work and that of absent colleagues. It is rather like an engine continually running at its optimum performance with no service break; when it is pushed further it becomes less reliable and then rapidly breaks down, usually at the most inconvenient time.

Reporting in November 2004, according to a joint review by the Ministerial Task Force for Health, Safety and Productivity and the Cabinet Office, 'long-term absence (particularly stress related) appears to have deteriorated in recent years: the percentage of individuals experiencing spells of long-term (21+ day) absence has increased from 5% in 2001 to 5.7% in 2003 – 44% of all days lost.'

What happens when one experiences distress?

There are numerous physiological changes in a full-scale stress response which may induce mental, emotional and behavioural changes. The individual may become more alert, angry or aggressive. The body will be energised by sugars and fats being released from the liver into the bloodstream so that quick bursts of energy are available. Respiration will become faster to bring more oxygen into the blood. The heart will beat faster to distribute the oxygen and blood pressure will increase so that muscles can react to demands for action.

This response was appropriate in the stone age when we were routinely vulnerable to predators. It is less often appropriate today, although some occupations, such as military personnel in combat situations require it.

When a stress response is generated routinely in sedentary occupations it can lead to ailments such as hypertension, coronary thrombosis, migraine, peptic ulcers, and colitis. It is therefore important to recognise distress in yourself and those around you to prevent these illnesses because the body cannot maintain the alert state for long without short- or long-term harm. Our earliest ancestors hunted wild animals for food just to feed themselves and their families – they could not just pop down to the supermarket! In medieval times a journey of a few miles could have been fraught with considerable dangers and physical hardship.

Our ancestors would nevertheless have been quite grateful to be spared the pace of modern life with its media, social demands and competitiveness in the UK, increasing isolation from the family unit (see Further Resources section and useful websites relating to dealing with stress at work).

How can we avoid distress?

We cannot. However, we can learn techniques to keep distress to a minimum by increasing our coping strategies. We can also use eustress appropriately in our occupations to improve our performance and inspire others.

Avoiding excess stress

There are a number of strategies which have a preventive or moderating impact on stress becoming extreme in an individual:

- learning to be more dynamic under pressure regulating mood and energy
- better ability to optimise what is urgent and a priority
- learning to negotiate with others
- improving self-awareness to learn when to say 'no' more often
- setting boundaries in the day.

Coping with stressful situations

Spend some time thinking about the situations which you find personally stressful. These can be either at work or home. Once identified, consider ways in which you could make these situations less stressful. For instance, would being better prepared or more assertive reduce the level of stress you experience?

Would practising some relaxation techniques such as deep breathing help you cope more effectively? Consider the use of aromatherapy and planning in 'me time' into your busy schedule to wind down and reflect after a busy day. You may have to negotiate with members of the family so that they understand your needs as much as you understand theirs. Being clear now will really help when you are faced with this situation again.

Stress factors

Identify from the list (which is not exhaustive), which are the sources of stress for you now:

- relationship with boss
- relationship with colleagues
- insufficient work
- work overload
- making mistakes
- feeling undervalued
- time pressures
- promotion prospects
- being relocated
- taking work home
- pay

- policy administration
- lack of power and influence
- lack of consultation and communication
- job ambiguity
- top management being remote
- lack of rest breaks
- lack of meal breaks
- corporate culture

After reading the rest of the chapter you should reflect on your coping strategies for what you have identified and what you have learned from the case studies and suggestions for stress management.

Stress management case studies

The following two cases are at extremely different scales of complexity. The first is a personal case study of a professional individual who works from home. Read through this personal story and reflect on parallels in your own daily life.

Case study 1: Reflections on stress

Today I felt distressed. Life seemed just too complex, the pressures too large, and the mountains too high. This stress affected my thinking and feeling in a downward spiral of gloom.

As I think about writing this piece, I have a powerful urge to minimise the unpleasantness and avoid appearing weak. I know that as a 'strong, confident man', I'm not 'supposed' to talk about these feelings. Strong men don't want to just crawl in bed and cry, do they? And Emotional Intelligence 'experts' are definitely not 'supposed' to be depressed, right?

The last few days have been challenging. Nothing earth-shaking, and when I talk to people whose spouses are dying, and people whose companies are on the verge of bankruptcy, and people whose employees are stealing from them... my troubles seem so petty (am I minimising again?).

Still, it's been troubling for me, so my stress level has been high. My back's been aching, I've been tired, and I've had a hard time focusing. Nothing's been going right, and I didn't see that it was going to change. This pessimistic thinking was creeping in (notice the 'nothing' and 'never'). It's a fine line between stress and depression.

This 'fine line' is shaped by neurobiology. Because I was stressed, my cortisol level increased, and therefore my serotonin was inhibited. Serotonin is the 'happy chemical', and it creates contentment, or wellbeing. So as I became more stressed, I got to be in a 'worse and worse' mood. If I had stayed in stress, the effects would have been even stronger.

There are many different strategies for getting out of this downward spiral. Journalising, exercise, a change of scenery and humour all are recommended. I tried two different approaches today: weeding and listening. One of my realisations was that the pressure to 'get out of the bad mood' was actually interfering with my learning.

Weeding

One of the great benefits of working at home a lot is that I can wear my wireless phone headset and work while weeding a bit of the garden! Remember that if I'm coaching you. Today that was not enough, so eventually I went to the vegetable garden and *really* weeded.

The problem with this stress cure is you've got to have weeds. The benefit, of course, is your garden gets a make-over. I suspect there's some therapeutic quality to ripping unwanted weeds out – direct action, visible results. These are great for stress. For myself, I suspect the larger benefit is reconnecting with nature. With the pace of my work life, it's easy to spend days and weeks in front of the computer, in traffic, on aeroplanes, and in office buildings and hotels with no fresh air. I cease to be a human being, and become a component of the information age. Kneeling in the dirt and getting my hands in the soil is a powerful counterpoint.

I suspect the reconnection to nature calls forth something primal, human-as-animal, and no-nonsense. Still, it wasn't quite enough. Despite almost two hours of weeding today, I was not done with feeling stressed.

Listening

In the midst of feelings I didn't like (stress, anxiety, depression), I tried several strategies to get these feelings to go away. Then (again) I remembered that all feelings have value. This has been one of the biggest, most difficult lessons of EQ for me. Feelings have value, even feelings I don't like.

The weeding helped reduce the urgency of the feelings, but they were persisting. I forced myself to go for a walk, and was thinking about writing an article on how to manage feelings of stress ... and suddenly I just stopped (in the middle of the apple orchard), realising that I was avoiding the feeling.

I took a few minutes just to allow myself to feel stressed and depressed, and listen to those feelings. What were they telling me? What was the wisdom of these feelings?

I had two realisations:

1. There are a bunch of items under my control and direct influence that I have not been taking care of. For example, one contributor to the feeling of stress is financial, and I realised that I have not sent invoices out for several weeks. I've also been taking on projects that are not particularly rewarding and so I've been over-busy. In both of these examples the unpleasant feeling was an appropriate reminder to get my act together!

2. I have not been thinking enough about my real purpose. A driving sense of purpose is an incredible resilience asset – insurance against stress. But I'd slipped from 'doing my work because it truly matters' to 'doing my work because it's my job'. Perhaps this is a natural consequence of being busy, having to pay bills, etc., but again the unpleasant feelings were an appropriate response to my lack of focusing on what's truly important.

The two strategies – weeding and listening – have some common themes. Both have a component of reflection, and a component of direct action. These two dimensions seem paradoxical, and that's one of the wonders of being in touch with feelings. They are ripe with paradox.

I'm glad to report that today I feel 90 per cent more focused than yesterday, I've sent out three invoices, completed two projects that have been dangling over my head, and feel energised to get engaged in the next items on my list.

More importantly, though, I'm coming into today reconnected with a sense of purpose, and recommitted to listening with love and acting with accountability.

The second case study is centred on a police force which by its very nature has to help its employees deal with stress at work. Read through this case study and consider how your organisation is tackling occupational stress – an area of increasing litigation.

Case study 2: Occupational stress for organisations

The implication of occupational stress for organisations has been brought into sharp focus in recent years by a number of high-profile legal rulings and an increasing recognition that employers are responsible for the psychological, as well as the physical welfare of their employees.

Being a member of a Police Force is recognised as an occupation that is highly stressful. A variety of research has identified a range of operational situations that give rise to stress, such as:

- court appearances
- the delivery of sudden death notifications
- general organisational factors such as managerial support and work overload.

Perhaps even more relevant to EI are the emotionally charged situations that surround many, if not the majority, of the interactions police officers have with their 'customers'. Often they are victims of crime, have just been involved in some form of accident or are distressed because a child is missing. Alternatively they may have, or be suspected of, breaking the law and are even being arrested. Either way there is often an abundance of emotion for the officer to deal with and more often, the emotion that manifests itself most is anger.

This is an example of the application of Emotional Intelligence to situations where individuals can be at risk of harm. It is also an example of where a uniformed service has become aware that it can exacerbate the public's sensibilities when their *intent is the exact opposite*. Therefore they have created strategies and policies to reverse or reduce this potential risk.

Since the late 1990s, police forces in the UK have explored and used EI development for a number of reasons:

- risk management of incidents, disturbances, crime scenes and public events to make the uniform mean more than it did, reducing risk and shifting perceptions in at risk communities
- safety planning for victims of crime to reduce them being harmed
- stress management and work/life balance for police staff.

Risk management of incidents
Better outcomes result and matters do not escalate if uniformed Police staff are given the skills to reduce the risk of a situation becoming inflamed by their uniformed presence. There are similar cases from the military when they are operating abroad in cultures diverse to their own. Better outcomes are achieved if officers:

- are self-aware and self-managed
- know how to achieve rapport with members of the

public and accurately assess the emotional climate prevailing at the time
● use techniques, such as active listening, voice control, body language, that are empathic and objective.

Safety planning

This increases the self-awareness and self-management of victims of (usually) domestic crime and possibly also the EQ of perpetrators. Varying force to force, this is a structured methodology of consultation between victims and agencies to enable them to make better use of resources. This is in order to understand the risk posed by the suspect and increase the victim's safety and that of their children. A victim's safety plan utilises an effective investigation and risk assessment. This is to reduce repeat victimisation which is likely to be less sustainable should there be an absence of higher EQ in the attending officers.

Work/life balance for police officers

It is not only officers themselves who suffer as a result of their daily work, but the impact is also significant on loved ones, although often the triggers can be different. Police work has dangers inherent in the job which cause most problems, but the long hours and shift work, cancelled leave and unhealthy coping strategies employed by officers may become habits leading to failing physical health and wellbeing. A high proportion of the longer term absences are as a direct result of stress-related illness. Government is under pressure to reduce the number of health-related early retirements within the police service.

Thus entire communities can be transformed by the greater emotional intelligence of participants in each community leading to true co-creation of social change; members of the public, emergency services, local and regional government, etc.

Emotional Intelligence development solutions need to address much deeper psychological issues and the specific emotional aspects that characterise the world of work. To be likely to experience lower levels of stress in working lives, interventions need to be designed to develop emotional competencies demonstrating an all round improvement in performance. Therefore, each could learn to better understand and manage their emotions and those of others, particularly anger.

Accordingly the overall objectives for the intervention were:

- to heighten awareness
- to increase knowledge
- to change attitudes and behaviour
- to offer the opportunity to improve quality of life, reduce the risk of illness and improve productivity.

A series of one-day workshops were offered to all those officers, and support staff members, who regularly had face-to-face contact with the public within the division (around two hundred staff). The workshops incorporated a range of experiential exercises (meditation, visualisation and biofeedback) lectures and questionnaires. The topics covered were:

- the causes and consequences of stress
- biological and emotional responses to stress
- stress coping strategies (perception, problem and emotion-focused)
- anger management (meaning, categories, sources, function and coping strategies).

The study

In order to explore the link between stress and Emotional Intelligence following the workshops, a sample of 100 officers, who had been amongst those invited to participate in the workshops, were asked to complete two questionnaires. The first was the Boston Emotional Intelligence Questionnaire™ based on the work of Weisinger (1998), who defines EQ as:

- self-awareness
- managing emotions
- self-motivation
- relating to others
- emotional mentoring.

The Boston EIQ was designed to measure the extent to which officers could understand and manage their emotions.

The second was a general lifestyle questionnaire developed to assess the current perceived stress levels of officers and the extent to which their lifestyle indicated their risk of suffering from stress. Whilst participants were asked to respond to the EQ using the work context, the stress questionnaire was designed to access information that would take into account broader lifestyle factors such as the wider family and environmental world of individuals (Hart, 1990; Lazarus, 1999).

The areas covered by this questionnaire can be briefly summarised as follows:

- current level of stress
- extent of anxiety
- perceived level of life/work success
- daily diet
- workload
- exercise
- physical symptoms related to stress

- work/life relationships
- user of external stimulants
- concerns/challenges faced.

The sample comprised 18 female and 82 male officers. All were operational 'front-line' staff working on patrol or in specialist posts (dealing with drugs offences for example), all within a busy inner-city environment. Of the 100 participants, 86 were constables and 14 held the rank of sergeant. The officers in the sample varied in their length of service from less than two years to almost thirty, and in age profile from 23 years to 54 years.

The findings and implications for stress management practitioners

Amongst the sample a strong correlation was found overall and between each of the five EQ abilities (self-awareness, managing emotions, self-motivation, relating to others and emotional mentoring) and lower levels of stress, emotion management showing the strongest relationship. In essence what the study revealed was that those front-line operational police officers that were able to understand and manage their emotions, reported lower levels of stress and were, according to their reported lifestyles, at less risk of suffering from stress in the future. These results were evident across the sample with no real differences evident regarding the age, gender rank or length of service of the officers involved.

Matthew and Zeidner (2001) suggest that successful coping with stressful encounters is central to Emotional Intelligence. So in the light of these findings what implications does this have for stress management practitioners? Firstly, it suggests EQ can be developed and makes a difference to the experience of stress. Secondly, widening our view of the experience of stress within the broader context of emotions generates a real prospect for stress management practitioners to develop interventions that make a real difference to the quality of working life. It offers a real possibility of re-humanising organisations, fit to house the human spirit.

Stress management strategies using EI

There is always a pay-off for unproductive behaviour (getting to be right, making someone wrong, playing victim or victimiser, dominating someone or being dominated and not responsible, invalidating the feelings of others, being invalidated, etc.). The cost of the bad behaviour is also all the self-negating behaviours – low self-esteem and so on.

> Review your self-observations and create a model of your behaviour. Describe in your own words what transition you need to make to eliminate your stress-inducing behaviour. Think of words to illustrate the beneficial and positive pay-off for you in making the change. You need to make the transition steps as achievable as possible. You also need to be sufficiently dissatisfied with the status quo. Think of the stress-related illnesses that could result from continuing your present pendulum swings over a long period of time. Note the disadvantages that would result. What might you have to stop doing that you enjoy? Replace those things which you enjoy now that are bad for you with things that give you joy and are good for you.

Like risk, stress is a perception and therefore highly personal. You need to differentiate between eustress and distress (good and bad stress). Distress is created through repeated negative behaviours. A pressure that is commonplace to one individual may be a huge source of stress for another.

Here are a series of checklists of stress management measures which, by managing what we cannot avoid and by eliminating what we can, will lead to better health ... leading you to take an EI approach to reducing stress.

Manage your relationships

- Have authentic, emotionally intelligent relationships with people. Associate with those whose company you enjoy and who support you. Authenticity requires self-awareness and emotional expression so that when in conversation with an individual you are able to share your feelings openly, including any distractions impairing your ability to concentrate on them. The relationship should be equitable and based on a sense of mutuality. Whilst the degree of give and take may vary from time to time based on your needs, it should find an agreed equilibrium. When worries start to build up, talk to someone with whom you have a close relationship.

- Learn how to have assertive conversations with those who create anxiety by not acknowledging your feelings and rights. As much as possible, clear your life of people who drain your emotional battery creating unacceptable anxiety and conflict. Don't drift along in troublesome and distressing situations or relationships. Take action to change rather than trying to avoid the problem or deny it exists. Taking chances is the key to emotional wellbeing.

- Protect your personal freedoms and space. Do what you want and feel, but respect the rights of others. Don't tell others what to do, but if they intrude, let them know.

- Set up a co-coaching relationship with someone you trust, preferably someone with coaching experience. Meet at least once a month, split the time and have a scheduled telephone call every week. Select life-improving books to read and share together. Tackle real issues, including denial and avoidance, with each other. Consider using a journal, to prepare for the co-coaching sessions, writing the results up at the time and after reflection.

- Watch your conversations for faulty thought patterns, such as selective envy, disaster forecasting, finding the scapegoat, generalisation and projecting our reactions onto others.

Manage your environment

- For one week, take note of changes to your stress levels and the environment you are in at the time.
- Being ruthless, identify the stressors and think what you can do about them (for example, clutter in the house, shed and garage, or your journeys to work, or the lack of a study or 'den' for you).
- Surround yourself with cues from positive thoughts and relaxation.
- Find a time and place each day where you can have complete privacy. Take time off from others and pressures.

Manage your lifestyle

- Change your lifestyle by removing the causes of stress.
- Effective time management is just one of many ways to keep from succumbing to stress overload (see Polly Bird, *Instant Manager: Time Management*). Make time to learn and practise relaxation or meditation skills.
- Engage in a vigorous physical exercise that is convenient and pleasurable. Check with your doctor before engaging on a new programme if you are unused to it. Sometimes it helps to get a friend to exercise with you to keep the discipline. Go to a gym or fitness centre with instructors

with recognised qualifications. Always do their induction session.

- Short breaks during the day (every 45 minutes if working at a computer) can help improve efficiency and wellbeing for the rest of the day. In addition, the breaks help with avoidance of problems with posture (lower back syndrome), eyesight and repetitive strain injuries (RSI).

- Maintain a reasonable diet and sane sleeping habits. Use alcohol and medication wisely – you must be in control of them and not vice versa. Avoid the use of sleeping pills, tranquillisers and other drugs to control stress (exercise really helps with sleeping problems as does a diet that acknowledges foods that can stimulate you throughout the day or encourage sleep at night)

Manage your attitude

'We are not upset by things but rather the view we take of them.'
Epictetus

You may have a positive attitude to something that is causing you and others around you stress. It may be a weakness because of its extreme nature when it could be moderated and become a strength. Apart from the need to balance life and career, our personal characteristics play an important role in creating stress. Seek the view of others on the characteristics that might add to your stress, such as:

1. perfectionism
2. misdirected anxiety
3. need for approval of others
4. pessimism
5. impatience

6. a wish to avoid conflict
7. poor opinion of self
8. misplaced optimism.

If we wish to avoid undue stress we must recognise the role such characteristics play and be prepared to modify our values.

An EI approach to reducing stress

You might want to experiment to see what works best for you. The features of an emotionally intelligent approach that can tackle stress are:

- increasing competencies in self-awareness, self-control and in awareness of others
- viewing life as challenges to seek and not as obstacles to avoid – review your obligations from time to time and make sure they are still good for you; if they're not, let them go
- using assertiveness through a balance of responsive and assertive behaviours
- identifying positive approaches to events, rather than just worrying with negative thoughts
- understanding the true cost of our values and beliefs
- not becoming one-dimensional – don't let one thing dominate you, such as a current project, schoolwork, relationships, career, sports, hobby, etc.
- open yourself to fresh experiences (try new fangled things, novel foods and new places); take responsibility for your life and your feelings, but never blame yourself – ownership of your life is a better philosophy than a blame culture.

INSTANT TIP

Make a stress management contract with yourself and, if you like, your staff. List what you need to start, stop and manage more effectively.

09

How does EI help conflict resolution?

Things to understand about getting into conflict

'It is not what people do that is the most interesting, it's why they do it.'

Dr Ros McCarthy

It is also the meaning that we apply to events which set rules up for our behaviour in the future. The following case study is an example of a leader who had trust issues with women especially female authority figures.

Case study: Conflict

The head of this significant UK organisation was in his fifties. There was a tragic incident in childhood which had affected him deeply. He had a bike that went a bit wonky and the steering became erratic. He loved his bike but his mother knew it was too small for him and it was showing signs of wear and tear. There was a family in the street less well off than them. His mother bought him a new bike and gave the old one to the family. He had warned his mother about the defect. The poor steering went unfixed. One day it contributed to the youngest daughter veering into the road and she was killed in a road accident. He had loved that little girl and he never forgave his mother for the loss.

A technique known as root-cause analysis can be helpful here in which the question 'why?' is asked five times until the source of the issue is exposed:

1. *Why was the girl killed?*
   She got into the path of an oncoming vehicle and was fatally injured.
2. *Why was she using a defective vehicle near traffic?*
   She was insufficiently supervised for her age and capability at the time.
3. *Why did she get into the path of the vehicle?*
   She was an inexperienced road user, cyclist, and the steering was faulty leading to her going off the pavement by her front yard.
4. *Why was the bicycle faulty?*
   The family could not afford a repair at the time and she had taken the bike from the garage where it was awaiting repair.
5. *Why did she do this?*
   She was thrilled at being given a bike and just could not wait to go out on it. She was just a little girl and naturally curious. Her parents were momentarily distracted by their other offspring when she slipped outdoors.

What our subject had *made* it mean in later life was twofold:

- Women do not listen to me, especially women with authority over me.
- Women cannot be trusted and harm will come to me or those I love.

In other words, this had become a limiting belief which guided his ability to be open to possibilities in relationships with women. He had had a tough climb to the top and acted out the 'female authority figure issue' regularly.

Recently he had had a clash with a newly promoted ethnic woman at work. She had had misunderstandings with him over leadership style, communication and motivation. His organisation arranged for him to work with a coach on this issue. The coach deconstructed the roots to his irrational assumptive behaviour with women. She established:

- he was not a male chauvinist
- he was not a racist
- he liked working with women and found the diversity strengthening
- he was working from an emotional path set up in the unresolved trauma in childhood.

Can you see that it was now possible for him to get into conflict without understanding why he would behave the way he did?

The coach helped him retrieve the emotional records of the event, the run-up to it and later ramifications. The emotions that he felt at the time were complex:

- He felt mildly jealous that the bike he still loved and which had given him much joy now belonged to another.

- He felt thwarted that his better judgement had been ignored and the bike had not been fixed before it was passed on.
- He was gutted that his childhood sweetheart had died this way and still mourned her loss. His grieving was incomplete; he had not accepted her death and moved on.
- He was still angry with his mother and yet he was sad that their relationship was coloured by the trauma.
- He had transferred this cocktail of emotions to all future relationships with women in authority.

Unless we delve into the emotional roots to our behaviour we are doomed to misunderstand why we do things. We need specific strategies to identify as foresight situations which may have pitfalls for us. This allows us to rehearse our responses.

OK, life is not a rehearsal, I hear you say. However, how good does it feel to have to constantly act from hindsight – reflect and repair? How awkward is it to catch yourself in the middle of creating or sustaining conflict with someone? Are some people in your life exhausted by the constant repair work in relationships? Unless you get to these roots you are doomed to this behaviour for life. Choose how you want to be – proactively.

How do you see this drama playing out then? Well, imagine that our subject calls a meeting between himself and his female colleague with a facilitator. The woman was not looking forward to this key conversation.

Our subject opens the conversation with an explanation of his childhood trauma and how this had been injected into their first few interactions in her new role. The woman, despite being very self-contained and prepared for conflict, is moved by his story. He elaborates on the impact it had on his mother. Long after her death he recognised her struggle, being abandoned by his father with this very intelligent little boy to raise on her own. It had been very hard for her to get the necessary resources to educate her gifted son. She had spent less time with him than she would have liked because she had to hold down several jobs to pay for extra tuition for him. She was herself very bright but poorly educated. She had always wanted to do Higher Education. She sacrificed that for him. The stress and strain of her situation led to cancer and a premature death.

- How could it have been different for his mother?
- How could their parent–child relationship have played out?
- How can it be different for him now?
- How can it be different with his colleagues and this newly promoted female colleague in particular?

After you have read the rest of the chapter, work out your own idea of facilitating this session or being one or other of the participants.

The games we play

We often feel trapped into patterns of behaviour or are utterly oblivious that we are racing down a well-trodden path to self-destruction or serious issues with relationships. It is useful to identify the answers to the following:

1. What is it that happens over and over again?
2. How does it start?

3. Then what happens?
4. What happens next?
5. How does it end?
6. How do you feel when it ends?
7. How may the others feel when it ends?

The Karpman Drama Triangle

Steve Karpman was writing about how drama roles get acted out within fairy stories when he drew what has become perhaps the best-known diagram from Transactional Analysis (in the *TA Bulletin*, of 1966).

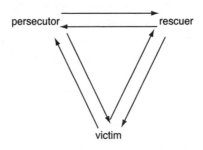

Figure 9.1: The Karpman Drama Triangle

In the game the players start in their familiar favoured position. When one of the players switches roles the game is completed. This simple diagram (Figure 9.1) demonstrates how we occupy one of three roles:

● **Victim**: Hopeless, helpless, and powerless, beyond the reality. 'You can make me feel bad or good'.

- **Rescuers**: Appear nice and helpful. 'I can make you feel good'. A person is rescuing when he or she:
  - is doing something he/she doesn't want to do
  - is doing something he/she was not asked to do
  - is doing something he/she can't do
  - is doing more than 50% of the work
  - is not asking for what he/she wants.
- **Persecutor**: 'I can make you feel bad'. People frequently take up the persecutor role in order to avoid being the victim.

Think of situations where individuals are portraying themselves as a victim and you feel drawn to rescue them.

- At some point did the situation flip and you became persecuted by one or more participants?
- What behaviour change did you notice in the victim?
- How did you feel when their behaviour shifted?

You need to work with others on the basis of adult-to-adult transactions and not get flipped into the drama triangle. Think of situations and relationships where this may be a familiar pattern for you. The next section illustrates some useful techniques to avoid this.

If you want to explore this more then read the work of Eric Berne the founder of Transactional Analysis (see Further Resources).

Three perceptual positions

In many business situations, the ability to look at a subject from a number of different perspectives can greatly add to the amount of information we have on a given subject, and can help us in making better choices and decisions.

In fact, it is useful not only to see things from different perspectives, but also to hear different arguments and get to grips with things from different positions. In addition, by acting as if we are someone else and viewing the situation from their position:

- we can also imagine that we hold their beliefs and values
- we know what problems they are dealing with
- we can begin to understand what motivates them.

We can therefore form a very complete idea of how that person may act and react to things we say and do. This skill provides you with top quality information.

There are three perceptual positions that we use to do this:

- **First position**: considering things from your own point of view.
- **Second position**: considering the situation from the point of view of being the other person – that is, stepping into their shoes and seeing, hearing and feeling the situation from their position. This involves you in imagining you hold their beliefs and values. This is an excellent way to judge the feelings of another person.
- **Third position**: seeing things from the point of view of a detached observer who is outside the situation. Imagine you are flying above the situation and looking down on it. From this position you have no ego-involvement or feelings about what is happening at all. From this 'meta' position you can ask questions like:
  - What is happening in this situation?
  - Is there anything that the person in first position has missed?
  - How does the person in second position feel?
  - What does the person in first position need to do now?
  - What's the next step to achieve the outcome you want?

The impact of EI on forming teams

Experience teaches managers that in forming a team, there has to be a storming stage before people settle down into performing well together.

Stages of team formation

1. **Forming**: a set of people come together for a specific purpose. Alternatively one or more new members join an existing team which has to form again as a result.
2. **Storming**: individuals discover the diversity in their colleagues and are not equipped to deal with it or understand how to use it beneficially. Controversy, frustration, miscommunication and disagreement can result.
3. **Norming**: the utility of differences emerges in using individuals and achieving outcomes.
4. **Performing**: the team gets a buzz about them and they know how to tackle work together using different talents and knowledge.
5. **Mourning**: team members miss each other when the team is disbanded. You know that you have got it right in building a team if this stage is reached.

Additional competencies for EI and conflict resolution?

Constructive discontent

Key to achieving the optimal output of group meetings is the use of constructive debate; this uses the emotional intelligence competence of constructive discontent.

The opposite of constructive discontent is 'destructive content'. The use of the word 'content' here means happy, satisfied, comfortable and at ease. The use of the word 'destructive' is intended to convey how futile it can be for teams to not debate issues thoroughly. Therefore, meetings can occur that resolve nothing and involve no commitment from individuals to a course of action. How many times have you sat in a meeting and noticed something going on but decided not to rock the boat and let it go on. Strong leadership relies on strong constructive discontent. You must build in mechanisms to listen to opposing views.

Definition: Your ability to stay calm, remain focused and be emotionally grounded in the face of disagreement or conflict. (Can you maintain balance even in the midst of disagreement?)

A manager with this competence:

1. looks at the degree of openness to hear another point of view and to suspend judgement
2. looks at the valuing of inclusion and your ability to tolerate ambiguity

3. looks at your skill in staying balanced when there is conflict versus reacting to the behaviours unproductively
4. knows your emotional triggers and uses skills to deal with them
5. has ability to invite opposite ways of thinking and disagreement without fear or worry that you will be pulled off your mark.

Think of a situation of conflict in your organisation:

● What happened?
● Were you the difficult person?
● How did you respond to antagonism if others tried to provoke you or other people?
● How did the leader handle it if that was not you?
● What does it feel like to stay in control when there is conflict around you?
● If you did not manage self-control, did you catch yourself in the act or do you agree you are in a 'reflection and repair' situation?
● If you did not achieve an ideal outcome, what can be salvaged from what occurred?
● What have you learned from this event?

What do I need to do to get better at conflict resolution?

Conflict-handling styles

There are two main ways that conflict-handling style varies from person to person:

1. **Determination to get your own way**: you might be assertive, pressing to meet your own needs, or you could be non-assertive, not pushing your aims too hard.
2. **Willingness to help others**: you could be co-operative, concerned to help other people meet their needs, or you might be uncooperative, not bothering about what others want.

These are not necessarily opposites. They come together in different combinations, giving the four styles that correspond to the four scores in the table:

	Uncooperative in meeting needs of others	Co-operative in meeting needs of others
Assertive in meeting own needs	Style D DETERMINED	Style C COMPROMISING
Non-assertive in meeting own needs	Style A AVOIDING	Style B BOUNTIFUL

Table 9.1: Conflict handling styles

There is not a universally 'best' style. You need to use all of them at some time or other. To some extent you will be responding to the other person's style interacting with you. The four styles are described as follows:

Style A – avoiding

Avoiders think the conflict cannot be resolved satisfactorily so it's best not to get involved. They say things like:

- 'Sorry, I can't help there.'
- 'You'd better ask my boss.'
- 'I've no idea – sorry.'

When is it best to avoid? Obviously there are cases that should be dealt with by your boss. The policy may be that in certain situations you must escalate issues. Perhaps you feel that you have not got the knowledge or experience to deal with the problem fully. Sometimes you are dealing with someone who is unstable – you can't get a satisfactory outcome no matter what you do, so avoiding makes sense.

Style B – bountiful

The bountiful person's motto is 'the other person is always right' – even when they are wrong. Everything possible is done to meet other people's needs and to agree with their views – even though it means inconvenience to the bountiful one.

When is it best to be bountiful? There may be cases where you have instructions always to give someone else the benefit of the doubt. This applies especially if the cost to you is small compared with the goodwill you will create. For example, when someone complains that you were all late starting, there is no point in disagreeing – even if you know the individual is wrong.

Style C – compromising

The compromiser aims for a 'win/win' outcome where neither party gets his or her own way entirely, but both sets of needs are met in essentials. The compromiser says: 'I'll do this if you'll do that.'

When should we compromise? More to the point, when can we? Often the rules we work under tie us down, and manoeuvring room is needed in order to arrive at a compromise. Both sides must be given something in return for getting what is essential. Often we need to say something to help cushion the other person to feel able to back down without losing face. ('I can see how it happened,' we say; 'Perhaps the instructions aren't as clear as they might have been.')

Normally, we have to compromise when it really does matter that both the other person's needs and our needs are met. But to arrive at such a solution, the other person must be prepared to compromise as well.

Style D – determined

If we are determined, we set out to win – even if this means getting other people to admit they are at fault, making them unhappy.

When should we be determined? Only when there is no alternative; when it is important not to make any concessions. For example, if a customer at a petrol station says the pump showed £5 at the start of delivery, the cashier cannot just take the customer's word for it (bountiful), or split the difference (compromising) if they know the customer is wrong. The cashier has to convince the customer that they are wrong. This needs time, tact and lots of information – but the cashier's got to win in the end.

Developing our style

There are two key points to make here:

- We all have our own preferred style.
- We need to use a range of styles in the job.

Which are your less preferred styles? When might they be useful to you? What will you do to develop them?

Stages in conflict

Conflicts at work often take time to develop. They come about from our perceptions of other people or of situations, and those are typically based on experience built up over a period of time. We are capable of raising our self-awareness when a stage has been reached or another has replaced it and choose to change our perceptions and attitude to work situations. This opens up greater self-management and awareness of others and engenders better management of relationships.

Suspicion

The first stage is often based on our suspicion that a conflict is arising. This suspicion may arise from someone's body language as they approach, such as that of an angry customer, or it may be from our experience of someone in a particular situation. For example, we may know we have always had a problem in getting our boss to let us have the Friday off before our annual holiday.

Evidence

In many cases we will wait and seek evidence to confirm or deny our suspicion – more often seeking that which will confirm the suspicion! Once we have enough evidence to confirm our suspicion, we will decide how we are going to react.

Retreat

We may decide immediately that we are going to avoid the conflict. We may do this by running away, denying the conflict exists. This can be an entirely appropriate response where the issues are unimportant, or where we feel a 'cooling-off' period is needed.

Alternatively, we may retreat by trying to smooth things over, once again trying to pretend the problem isn't really there. We tend to adopt this approach when we believe that maintaining a relationship is more important than the problem itself.

Attack

Not being ones to run away from conflict, we tackle it head on. We use our power and authority to achieve a solution, usually our own! Like most aggressive approaches, this may get compliance but any unwilling compliance will store up future problems. We force the other person to retreat.

Guerrilla war

We may sometimes decide that a frontal attack is not the best approach. Maybe we lack the power, or maybe we believe the direct approach will generate too strong a defence.

We therefore adopt an alternative approach of a guerrilla war: wearing our opponent down bit by bit until, we hope, they eventually see our point of view. However, guerrilla wars often last a long time. Even if we force a retreat on this occasion, we may find ourselves fighting another guerrilla war at every future encounter with that person or department.

Sometimes what starts as a guerrilla war develops into a direct attack from either party to the conflict and things get very uncomfortable indeed.

Negotiate

The two parties get together to collaborate in resolving the problem between them. Neither may get everything they seek but the aim is to agree a common goal that will satisfy both parties: a win/win goal.

For the agreement to work both parties must be committed to it. Neither party must feel that they have 'lost out'. If either party feels that they have given up too much, the compromise solution is unlikely to last and could easily end up in guerrilla war.

Dealing with anger

Many of us have difficulty in coping with people who are angry. We may fight back. We may try to escape the anger by running away from it, mentally if not physically. Neither of these responses will deal with the underlying situation that is giving rise to the anger.

In disarming anger we have two objectives:

- To calm down the other person and dissipate the anger. It is not possible to discuss a problem rationally while emotions are heavily involved.
- To resolve the underlying problem so that it will not occur again.

The techniques

Keep calm

Make sure you do not panic or lose your own temper – easy to say, but not always easy to do. If you lose self-control, you are less likely to dissipate the other person's anger in order to move on to resolving the problem.

Listen

Pay full attention so you can gather as many facts as possible as well as identifying any other underlying feelings that have generated the anger.

Empathise

Make sure that you acknowledge your understanding of the other person's views and feelings. Agree with whatever you honestly can agree with, including admitting the possibility that you might be part of the problem if that is the case.

Some typical responses that can be used to show empathy are:

- 'Yes, I can see how angry you are.'
- 'I can understand that you feel that way.'
- 'What exactly did she say?'
- 'It has been going on a long time, hasn't it?'
- 'Yes, I didn't get it finished on Friday as I had hoped.'
- 'Maybe I didn't give enough thought to that possibility.'
- 'I'm glad you're telling me about this.'
- 'I want to try to resolve it with you.'

You may well recognise that these responses are using some of the classic techniques of assertive behaviour: reflective statements, negative enquiry, negative assertion and fogging.

Don't argue

Until the anger and any other emotions are out of the way, there is no point trying to use logical, rational argument. It is only likely to fuel the anger.

Try to solve the problem

Once the anger is dissipated, try to move on to the resolution of the problem with phrases such as: 'OK, now let's see what we can do to sort it out between us.'

Save face

You need to do this throughout the discussion by:

- agreeing with what you can
- focusing on the problem, not the personality
- avoiding 'yes', but using 'I' instead of 'you'.

The techniques of assertive behaviour should respect your rights whilst not violating the rights of others. The need to save face may be particularly strong in many cultures once the chemistry of anger has dissipated. Many people experience remorse in hindsight. They then feel guilty about their loss of self-control or foolish for having lost their temper or the extent to which they had gone 'over the top'. Use reflective, non-judgemental and empathic statements such as:

- 'Yes, you did go a bit over the top but I can well understand why.'
- 'We all get angry at times and it helps to get the emotion out of the way so we can then tackle the problem together.'

Make sure that you accurately reflect the feelings the other person is expressing, and that what you say is honest and in no way patronising.

Three types of behaviour

Submissive

Submissive (or non-assertive) behaviour means not standing up for ourselves, giving way to other people, expressing our views in a cautious or timid way. The disadvantage of this type of behaviour is that our own views are ignored and our wishes neglected. As a result, we may become resentful, lose confidence in ourselves, or feel our efforts are not properly appreciated.

Aggressive

Aggressive behaviour is at the other end of the scale from passive or submissive behaviour. We go in absolutely determined to make our views heard and to get our own needs met solely. If our approach inhibits other people from expressing their views, or meeting their needs, so be it. It is up to them to fight their own corner.

The disadvantage of this type of behaviour is that any gains we make are likely to be short-term ones, even if we get what we want on this one occasion.

Assertive

Often confused with being demanding and used in a negative way when describing people, assertive behaviour is that which is aimed at meeting our own needs as well as possible, whilst respecting the views and needs of other people, both tangible needs for material things and any unmet emotional needs in a relationship. At best we do not feel anxious about expressing our own views or standing up for our rights. It is done in such a way that it does not threaten or punish other people. We deal openly and fairly with other people.

Causes of submissive behaviour

Here are some typical causes:

- wanting to be liked and to avoid upsetting someone
- avoiding the fear of unpleasantness or conflict
- avoiding the fear of being wrong and its consequences
- not wanting to seem aggressive
- not knowing how to stop being submissive or passive.

Add any other causes you know of for submissive behaviour and notice how many of these causes come from inside us: our self-doubt and our inner fears.

Causes of aggressive behaviour

Some typical causes of aggressive behaviour are:

- fear of being seen as weak
- liking to be feared – there is a visceral pay-off
- it's worked in the past – you got your own way
- through experiencing emotional upset or stress, possibly from frustration
- enjoying a good fight
- fear of being proved wrong
- don't know how to be assertive without perceiving it as being submissive.

Add any other causes you know of for aggressive behaviour and observe how most causes are internally generated.

Remember that no one type of behaviour suits all circumstances. Assertive behaviour is often the best approach but not always. Sometimes you may be best advised to adopt a submissive role. As the saying goes, 'He who fights and runs away, lives to fight another day.' Alternatively, it may be in your best interests to accommodate someone else's needs at the expense of your own wishes.

Do not rely solely on one style. The psychologist Abraham Maslow is quoted as saying: 'If the only tool you have is a hammer, everything else in the world will look strangely like a nail.'

Be prepared to choose the right behaviour for the particular circumstances which will usually, but not always, be assertive.

Summary

Try not to fear anger. See it as an emotional barrier to problem-solving that is best expressed so that the barrier disappears. Very few people can remain angry for long if there is nothing to fight against.

1. Continuously improve your self-awareness and be self-questioning. For example, ask yourself 'Who is actually being difficult here?'
2. Learn techniques for diffusing conflict.
3. Encourage debate and commitment to decisions.
4. Learn facilitation skills for group situations.
5. Learn different styles of leading groups which span democratic, participative styles to the more directive visionary styles. Avoid coercive behaviour.
6. Learn how to be a good Chairperson getting the best out of meetings and the people attending.

INSTANT TIP

Describe hidden agendas at work and identify what you can say openly about the issues. Rehearse your comments considering the reactions of others and then confront the situation.

10

How does EI fit with diversity?

What is diversity?

Diversity is about inclusion when recognising differences, not exclusion because of them. Diversity is a buzzword these days, although a variety of meanings are attributed to it in the workplace. In common parlance, it means we are a mixed bag by our natural divergence from one another and our individual distinctiveness.

We have probably more similarities than differences. However, as human beings, finding common ground is a good starting point to engender tolerance leading to collaboration as opposed to conflict. From the rapport and empathy gained in this process, there is a climate of inclusion; acceptance of diversity and what it means can then be explored.

Definition: Variety and difference – the opposite of uniformity.

Measuring diversity

Primary dimensions of diversity

- age
- ethnicity/race
- sexual orientation
- gender
- physical ability
- communication and learning styles

The bulk of legislation forces companies of a certain size to create a workforce profile that closely mirrors demographics. However, such compliance does not lead to an organisational climate that embraces diversity as a strategic asset.

These primary dimensions are generally unalterable and are extremely powerful in their effects on people's perceptions, effective teamwork and workforce cohesion.

Secondary dimensions of diversity

- geographic location (where you were born or currently live)
- travel to work complexity (affects who you can get to work there)
- income
- parental status
- marital status
- political affiliations and beliefs
- religious beliefs
- work experience

Secondary dimensions are significant influencers, but they are to some extent mouldable because we have choice in some and a measure of control over others.

What we notice

Research has shown that the nine most important things noticed about people in most societies, in order of importance, are the following:

1. skin colour
2. gender
3. age
4. appearance/style of dress
5. facial expression/accent
6. eye contact
7. movement/mannerisms
8. personal space
9. touch

Upon encountering one another:

- we notice fine details subconsciously
- we make assessments and judgements
- we make decisions about how to interact with one another based on these factors.

The first three items on the list (skin colour, gender and age) are virtually unalterable. They are extremely powerful in determining where we live and work, whom we socialise with at work, and even affect how much we earn.

Plenty of research evidence exists that shows how these differences crop up in the various human resource practices used in business life, such as appraisal ratings, rate of career progression and promotion in different geographic regions.

The last six on the list (appearance/style of dress, facial expression/accent, eye contact, movement/mannerisms, personal space and touch) are all culturally influenced.

In a multicultural organisation there are complex issues facing those people tasked with bringing about a cultural transformation to embrace diversity as a strategic business asset (and cope with the legal/political demands for diversity and transformation).

The obvious or surface level of culture, such as whether we give a handshake or a hug, a direct stare or lowered eyes, is determined by the culture we were raised in, and the primary and secondary dimensions of diversity.

Business culture emerges over time from the interaction between a company's current management and leadership practices delivering strategy. It is influenced at a tactical level by people management, monitoring and control systems. Misalignment leads to the mission going off-course.

Examples of organisational culture are:

- getting to know the rules of the game for getting ahead
- learning how far you can push managers before getting a 'black mark' allocated to your invisible scorecard which determines important project team placements.

All companies have an invisible cultural code (totally independent of diversity and transformation issues) called the 'right and the wrong way to do things around here'. Combine this dynamic with the primary and secondary dimensions of diversity and you have a very powerful force to reckon with when it comes to encouraging people to value diversity, let alone embrace it for strategic advantage.

> Ask yourself whether your company's culture is helping or hindering the creation of the right conditions for diversity to take root in the organisation.

If you are tasked with the job of auditing a diversity event, or your company's overall diversity strategy, remember to gather as many direct and indirect measures about these matters before drawing any meaningful conclusions.

Giving every identifiable group a 'piece of the action' is the most significant challenge presented. Becoming open to differences and creating an inclusive environment means that new groups will need to be placed in decision-making and influential positions. This feels uncomfortable and old groups feel vulnerable. It is rare to find examples of powerful individuals who willingly share their authority. Managing diversity in a meaningful way demands that business deals with this fundamental strategic issue, over and above paying attention to affirmative action and equitable employment practices.

How is diversity related usefully to EI?

The purpose of relating EI to diversity is to influence positively morale and workforce cohesiveness. As a manager you would want to get the best out of every individual, how they contribute to team work and the organisation's results.

You have to admit that there is often a degree of discomfort about something which is new to us that will impact our lives. If we are not prepared to attain a degree of collective discomfort we are unlikely to be innovative. Our need for the status quo will stifle creativity. Hence, the need to embrace diversity and walk the fine line between edgy discomfort and a comfort that stifles.

Ignoring diversity factors can lead to incomplete solutions for customers. Strengths can be overlooked and gaps not filled in the teamwork. Group EQ can be higher than the sum of the diverse individuals' EQ scores. Equally in the wrong organisational climate it can be lowered by the team dynamics and poor communication where the differences are not used to strengthen group process and outputs.

Working with people from different cultural backgrounds can be stimulating or problematic – it depends on our appetite for learning at a fundamental level. Certainly, some differences can be quite shocking to an individual when they are first noticed as we can work on assumptions which prove to be incorrect. We need to understand the organisational dynamics involved, and how these interplay with our own view of the world. If you are a manager trying to achieve and maintain optimal performance, then succeeding in this understanding is essential.

The workplace blend of nationalities, social customs, cultural differences and ethnicity (especially historically long-standing differences) tends to lead to inadvertent misunderstandings between managers and individual staff. For example:

1. Observation of people's actions and behaviour.
2. Interpretation of observed behaviours (within your own cultural view of norms).
3. Assignment of motive and meaning to the behaviour and actions of others without enquiry and dialogue leading to upset.

This can lead to delays or missed deadlines on projects, or sometimes staff leaving. It is a manager's responsibility to be free from judgement, accepting diversity as it manifests itself and to demonstrate this in their leadership style. This brings all the EI competencies to bear: self-awareness, social-awareness, self-management and relationship management. Suspending judgement on what is valued and accepted allows the manager to maximise innovation and creativity for greater productivity.

When people live in a climate of being judged there is a direct effect on trust in interpersonal relationships of the team. Trust is often a combination of sincerity, competence and reliability.

Cultural distrust stems from historical judgements – where different countries have equally legitimate realities. In these cultures, is the individual free to make their own judgement about whether we are insincere, incompetent or unreliable? There is a need to explore breaches of trust which have led to the individual not making up their own mind to make a positive assessment of trustworthiness.

Root cause analysis

Root cause analysis needs to be done by asking 'why?' five times until the source of the judgement is exposed or found to be missing:

1. Why are we judged as insincere? What is the evidence for it? (Five times asked and responded to with evidence of the disingenuousness.)
2. Why are we judged as incompetent? What is the evidence for it? (Five times asked and responded to with specific evaluative feedback on the perception of capability.)
3. Why are we judged as unreliable? What is the evidence for it? (Five times asked and responded to with specific occurrences of dependability being absent.)

An example of when this needs to be done would be a manager with a team that has been renewed in some way (new joiners or a new team role). If the manager is inexperienced, they may try to incentivise the team when there are unspoken issues or sources of dissatisfaction with the new role. This works against any model of human motivation. The emotionally intelligent thing to do is to recognise the emotional climate of the team when they are together and to specifically put the interpersonal relationships on the table for discussion.

What is the impact in the workplace as a manager?

It is important to understand that managers lead the organisational climate and it can be one that embraces diversity as a strategic asset. Innovation in organisations is only created by individuals sharing their initiatives. Each individual should be able to make a contribution, no matter how diverse from the mass thinking, be respected and be heard.

Embracing and capitalising on diversity goes far beyond equitable employment practices and affirmative action measures. The central issue in dealing with diversity is that power sharing is a business cultural and political matter. Unless the affirmative action on diversity includes power sharing then issues will rise to the surface to be dealt with by managers repeatedly. Your positive actions will not take root in the hearts and minds of staff. This means looking at decision-making (professional) and how judgements (personal) are formed.

Accepting diversity

So how do you have to *be* to bring the EI competencies together with the utility of accepting diversity into your own world?

1. Try being an anthropologist and develop your curiosity about inclusion and what is different or new.
2. Remember that maximising creativity generates innovation and therefore greater productivity, sharing initiatives of all people for profit and enjoyment.
3. Be innovative in a way that feels like you're on a fine line between 'edgy' and 'in discomfort'.
4. Accept diversity in all of its variety and beauty and see

the utility of it in that process. Recognise that it is a good idea for the diversity of your staff to match the diversity of your customer base. This should be welcome in a global economy and we should see that it is time to develop tolerance of our differences. We need to move towards and not away from our differences.

5. Look at the pragmatics of decision-making (professional) and the individual process of how judgements (personal) are formed.

You have seen in earlier chapters the cost of engendering low EQ within the organisation and the impact on customer transactions and the bottom line. Organisations that use its diverse components probably make better decisions and get more robust, rounded solutions than ones with more monotone or cloned components.

Emotions play a strong part in decision-making whether they are acknowledged or not. Decision-making varies with culture and ethnicity. Decisions are not made through sole use of the rational and logical side of the brain. We are going to look at a professional example of diversity and EI. Later we will look at a more personal and general example of making judgements in everyday life.

Planning the outcome

Say that you are in a situation where you have to make a big decision with someone new and different from you. You do not know a lot about this other person's culture or there is another aspect that makes you diverse. The following table sets out an effective strategy for exploring diversity issues in a simple self-help way by asking yourself these questions, or in a one-to-one way as in a coaching conversation. Obviously in a coaching situation the phrasing of the questions is done by the coach.

A Self-awareness	**B Social awareness**
How am I feeling? What emotion(s) am I feeling (emotional literacy)? How did these feelings emerge and what information arises from that?	What is the other person feeling? How can I check this out politely? How did they come to feel like that? How might those feelings change to achieve a greater outcome?
C Self-management	**D Relationship management**
What makes me lose concentration and the ability to manage myself with others (or this person, now)? What feelings do I want to have? What do I need to do to establish self-control and feel that way? How can I signpost this for myself in the future?	What is the best emotional outcome for this relationship? ● How do I want to feel at the end of this conversation? ● How do I want the other person to feel? ● What do I have to do to achieve this?

Table 10.1: Managing the emotional outcome

Start with the end in mind, by establishing the emotional outcome that you want to drive for, for example, a high degree of rapport or trust, a sense of being understood, respected or listened to and other positive outcomes such as agreement or concord.

For example, a client/coach dialogue demonstrates how a middle manager might assume certain behavioural characteristics are the same for everyone in the same working environment as himself, regardless of his colleagues' social or cultural background and conditioning. This leads him to misunderstand two younger and less experienced members of his team whose education and upbringing took place in India, where a different set of social, family and organisational values apply.

It takes a coaching intervention for this manager to appreciate that his interpretation of team members' behaviours around recent project events is just one perspective, and that it is vital for today's managers to understand, and preferably experience, the richness and diversity of international, multicultural working.

Adopting a multi-perspective approach, developing the ability to 'stand in the shoes' of colleagues whose cultures and backgrounds are different, and therefore to appreciate who our colleagues are and what they bring to the workplace is just as important and valid as appreciating our own individual perspective.

The subject of EI in development of people is still relatively new in the UK – although leading companies have been using EI competencies in their frameworks for a number of years. The bulk of companies are just beginning to catch on to their value in the employee lifecycle. Barbara Paterson (a very experienced consultant using EI assessments with foreign cultures) sees many appraisal systems that take a parental approach and do not result in the development that people need. Use of EI assessments combined with learning events and coaching can produce more effective outcomes.

Much of the early work centred on stress indicators, employee wellbeing and pressure management indicators (Kerry Cooper and Steve Williams in the late 1980s). The roots of the EQ Map™ are in the Occupational Stress Indicator work. One interesting point is that employee wellbeing should be part of the Quality Model of the company. Honda said that if you concentrated your effort on the quality of the experience at work and not on the outputs (as a manager) then you would achieve startling results.

It is possible for an experienced coach to evaluate a person's EQ without use of an instrument, through a series of carefully managed interventions. Questions can be asked of the individual as exercises conducted to elicit information about behaviour and its emotional or values-based roots. (See for example the questions in Chapter 14 of *SQ: Connecting with Our Spiritual Intelligence*, a book by Danah Zohar and Ian Marshall, Bloomsbury, 2000.)

With a well-schooled coaching style of leadership, EI culture change programmes can replace classic appraisal systems with a non-parental approach to 'slicing up the development cake' and to performance management. Appraisal systems do not give the development that people need. In a culture of high EQ, individuals are very positively motivated to their own learning and proactive about it. There are thousands of opportunities in most people's lives these days with the increase in Virtual Learning Resource Centres and e-learning spread through the Internet.

It will become increasingly important in the future to attract and retain good staff and to get the extra mile out of each employee. Great leadership practices are needed to get at the 30 per cent of effort that most people do not bring to work. Most people know that they could give more, not necessarily in the way of time but intellectually and creatively. Great coaches and leaders can get this out of people. This missing potential is doubly grave when it is added to the demographic trough in the 28–40 age range and shortage of 'gold collar' workers (i.e. MBAs). Everyone will be in competition and chasing the same talent. EI work aligned to values and competency frameworks can give companies the edge they need.

If you are in the position of increasing organisational EQ where there are multi-national as well as multi-cultural change issues, then the work of Fons Trompenaars (see Further Resources and following section) is relevant to what you are trying to achieve. Transcultural competence equals the propensity to reconcile seemingly opposing values. Whereas middle managers make decisions on issues, high-performing leaders and international managers continually reconcile dilemmas.

This is very different from achieving a compromise. Increasing EI through development events is directly relevant to taking people through the process of understanding and reconciling multi-cultural differences. Comprehending how different socio-cultural groups have strengths that can be used to benefit the organisation, the group and the individual not only celebrates diversity but is evidence of high EI. However, not all EI techniques transfer from one part of the world to another and care must be taken in design to cater for this.

Trompenaars' Seven Transcultural Competencies

Fons Trompenaars, Dutch author and specialist in the field of cross-cultural communication, challenges the assumptions that senior leaders operate on to continually reconcile dilemmas by use of his Seven Transcultural Competencies:

1. Common rules for all v. each situation is a 'one-off'; legal contracts v. loose interpretations; exporting v. multi-local; extending rules v. seeking exceptions.
2. Individual creativity v. group loyalty; rights v. duties; originating new (own) ideas v. refining useful existing products; individual v. team performance.
3. Bottom line v. goodwill; data and explicit knowledge v. conceptual models; stressing facts v. relationships.
4. Detached v. enthusiastic in the interaction; long pauses v. frequent interruptions; professional v. engaged.
5. Working for money v. working for status; status follows or precedes success; headhunting v. developing in-house.
6. Create new market v. satisfy existing markets; driven by own conscience v. outside influences; create your own strategy v. fuse with others.
7. Deadlines before quality v. quality above deadlines; step-by-step v. parallel processing; win the race v. shorten the course.

True globalisation of a multi-national organisation takes specific know-how. Managers need to:

● be aware of cultural differences
● respect those differences
● reconcile cultural differences and not accept compromise.

Test your propensity to generate a culture in your organisation as well as your proclivity to reconcile socio-cultural issues with your employees. Ask yourself:

1. What are the qualities that you identify as being important to you in the process of leading a change programme?
2. What kind of challenges would you need to face to be the kind of leader that you want to be?
3. Is there a development gap in the leaders of your organisation in the process of change?
4. What do you need to bridge this gap?

Case study: Diversity and EI

The following is a fictionalised case study constructed to illustrate points relating to diversity (competence in different cultures) and Emotional Intelligence (emerging ability). EI is awareness-based and sometimes even the most highly developed individuals can be pulled up short by what people do. Thus there is a need for emotional learning not just cognitive process.

The situation is one where an experienced consultant has been requested to 'parachute in' to take the place temporarily of a very experienced director of five investment retail and commercial banks in a group of companies. The bank is about to merge with another as part of a longer term strategy of withdrawal from the Caribbean region. The timing is days after 11 September 2001 and the director had staff involved in the terrible events of that day in New York. The coaching conversation takes place shortly after the return of the consultant to the UK having completed the interim assignment. It is part of coaching supervision for the consultant and continuous professional development.

The two global banking brands decided to merge their Caribbean operations. In many cases branches were on the same street on 25 Caribbean islands. Many had been established in the 1950s, and in some instances earlier. It was not solely retail banking either. Both banks had significant holdings in dealing with lucrative offshore banking services. This deeply profitable seam of trading was not to be prejudiced by the rationalisation of branches on the islands.

The most significant director was a man with enormous experience of changing cultures in the UK and the Caribbean . The coaching conversations covered:

- Some background information: history of colonialism and of course slavery (which has a big impact on trust); historic connections with the Caribbean.
- Social issues and the way they impact employment issues, leading to:
    - trust in relation to race (black v. white issues)
    - trust in relation to gender (male v. female issues – very different from the UK)
    - trust in employment (employee v. employer issues)
    - how and why Barbados is similar to and different from other Caribbean countries
    - attitudes to sexual preferences or predispositions

   – lingering attitudes to the legacy from slavery
     which limit freedom of indigenous black people
     and white Westerners.

Culture of the 25 islands and 15 territories

Culture is often hard to define but it can be simplified as the body of people's expressions, values, meanings and artefacts that anchor peoples' identity. Caribbean culture is identifiably linked to the approaches to survival taken by her peoples over the last 500 years.

Looking through the lenses of history and geography the Caribbean has lingering Imperial influences from the Dutch, French, Spanish, British, Americans and the Canadians. A number of islands were fought over, won and lost many times over. The resident population, including slaves, had to negotiate their survival against an ever-changing backdrop of politics and conquest. As you can imagine this history now manifests itself in an unwillingness to trust Westerners and Europeans too quickly. Equally, the legacy has resulted in different languages, Feast Days, holiday periods, traditions, laws and other practices.

The major ethnic groups of the region, namely the East Indians, Africans and European peoples, have maintained to varying degrees their ability to reconnect with their ancestral heritage. European traditions while they account in many respects for the official articulation of culture, are often supplanted by ethnic identity in many respects especially with relation to the majority African tendencies.

One size does not fit all

The two banks were led by North American (Canada and the United States) and British individuals, themselves poles apart culturally at times. Perspectives of culture and development from a Eurocentric perspective do little to seriously advance native Caribbean paradigms. Subsequently, a significant part of the change programme was designed to give voice to the non-Eurocentric viewpoint.

Visitors to the Caribbean have been known to assume that 'one size fits all' when it comes to local culture. Frequently, visitors' experience is of being waited on at poolside or beachside venues and offered every available sporting activity or entertainment. However, observing and asking the right questions, there are notable differences between the cultures on the islands:

- Trinidad and Jamaica have more in common with each other in the way they deal with business matters (quite bullish) than they would with locals in St Lucia or St Vincent (cautious, distant, polite).
- Guyana, Surinam, Dominica and Belize culture has an Amerindian presence seen through understated archaeological evidence of Tiano, Arawak and Carib peoples seen in caves and shown in Museums.
- Trinidad and Tobago and Guyana have greater identity with Asian cultural practices especially with respect to food, religion and the subsequent different worldview this engenders.

Common threads in Caribbean culture:

- Religion and superstition have varied cultural underlays that change their strictly 'Caribbean mono-cultural' character; Jonkanoo in the Bahamas, Santaria in Cuba, Voodoo in Haiti, and Rastafari in Jamaica are some examples. Some of these forms have been transferred from the Caribbean to the world such as Rastafari philosophy, reggae music, steel pan, Cajun and jerk cooking and regional rums and spices.
- The music of reggae and calypso, creative sources

of solace globalise the idea of Caribbean levity. The music is universally recognised as a cultural lingua franca for the African Diaspora. The emergence of Creole languages is perhaps one of the more clearly identifiable cultural forms to have emerged in the Caribbean explicitly preserving African, European, Asian ideas/words in the common everyday popular expression. Linguists have indicated that there are even connections between Jamaican patois and ancient Egyptian hieroglyphics.

- Culturally, the superstructure of the Caribbean islands embodies legacies of slavery. Still lingering is the economics of 'single' crop cultivation (sugar cane on Barbados for rum production), which still maintains the means of production in the hands of few privileged land owners. Sugar and banana plantation owners are the benefactors of such agro-economics and many workers still labour seasonally as they eke out a living. There is a growing Fair Trade initiative, however, politically the culture is of independent nations within a world system of Western interpretative democracy. The capitalist system of production is still the overarching economic culture and offshore banking is key to the economy of many islands replacing the plantation trade as the Gross National Product, closely followed by tourism.
- Story-telling forms a basis of cultural bonding, transferring wisdom, teaching the young and handling emotional topics (like HIV in co-workers).
- There are strong emotional bonds to brands; people actively grieved for their uniforms and their business cards and it was necessary to treat the change as a

shock. Being part of *that* branch and *that* brand was deep inside an individual's purpose and identity. Interventions had to be designed to take people though this grief curve and help them become happy members of staff living a new brand experience.

Differentiating cultures

Gerard Hendrik Hofstede (b. 1928), an influential Dutch writer on the interactions between national cultures and organisational cultures, developed a model that identifies four primary dimensions to assist in differentiating cultures: Power Distance Index (PDI), Individualism (IDV), Masculinity (MAS), and Uncertainty Avoidance (UAI). He added a fifth dimension after conducting an additional international study with a survey instrument developed with Chinese employees and managers. Based on Confucian dynamism, that dimension is Long-Term Orientation (LTO) and was applied to 23 countries. These five Hofstede Dimensions can also be found to correlate with other country and cultural paradigms.

- **Power Distance Index (PDI)**: the extent to which the less powerful members of organisations and institutions (like the family) accept and expect that power is distributed unequally. This represents inequality (more versus less), but defined from below, not from above. It suggests that a society's level of inequality is endorsed by the followers as much as by the leaders. Power and inequality, of course, are extremely fundamental facts of any society and anybody with some international experience will be aware that 'all societies are unequal, but some are more unequal than others'.
- **Individualism (IDV)**: individualism, on the one side,

versus its opposite, collectivism (the degree to which individuals are integrated into groups). On the individualist side we find societies in which the ties between individuals are loose: everyone is expected to look after him/herself and his/her immediate family. On the collectivist side, we find societies in which people from birth onwards are integrated into strong, cohesive in-groups, often extended families (with uncles, aunts and grandparents) which continue protecting them in exchange for unquestioning loyalty. The word 'collectivism' in this sense has no political meaning: it refers to the group, not to the state. Again, the issue addressed by this dimension is an extremely fundamental one, regarding all societies in the world.

● **Masculinity (MAS):** versus its opposite, femininity, refers to the distribution of roles between the genders which is another fundamental issue for any society to which a range of solutions are found. The IBM studies (conducted by Hofstede between 1967 and 1973) revealed that (a) women's values differ less among societies than men's values; (b) men's values from one country to another contain a dimension from very assertive and competitive and maximally different from women's values on the one side, to modest and caring and similar to women's values on the other. The assertive pole has been called 'masculine' and the modest, caring pole 'feminine'. The women in feminine countries have the same modest, caring values as the men; in the masculine countries they are somewhat assertive and competitive, but not as much as the men, so that these countries show a gap between men's values and women's values.

● **Uncertainty Avoidance Index (UAI):** deals with a society's tolerance for uncertainty and ambiguity; it ultimately refers to man's search for Truth. It indicates to what extent a culture programmes its members to feel either uncomfortable or comfortable in unstructured situations. Unstructured situations are novel, unknown, surprising, and different from usual. Uncertainty avoiding cultures try to minimise the possibility of such situations by strict laws and rules, safety and security measures, and on the philosophical and religious level by a belief in absolute Truth; 'there can only be one Truth – and we have it'. People in uncertainty avoiding countries are also more emotional, and motivated by inner nervous energy. The opposite type, uncertainty accepting cultures, are more tolerant of opinions different from what they are used to. They try to have as few rules as possible, and on the philosophical and religious level they are relativist and allow many currents to flow side by side. People within these cultures are more phlegmatic and contemplative, and not expected by their environment to express emotions.

● **Long-Term Orientation (LTO)**: versus short-term orientation. This fifth dimension was found in a study among students in 23 countries around the world, using a questionnaire designed by Chinese scholars. It can be said to deal with Virtue regardless of Truth. Values associated with Long-Term Orientation are thrift and perseverance; values associated with Short-Term Orientation are respect for tradition, fulfilling social obligations, and protecting one's 'face'. Both the positively and the negatively rated values of this dimension are found in the teachings of Confucius, the most influential Chinese philosopher who lived around 500 BC (however, the dimension also applies to countries without a Confucian heritage).

Your journey as a manager of other people may be one you have started somewhat reluctantly or with a deepening sense of possibility of natural progression for yourself and those in your charge. Remember that regardless of what you have been gifted as IQ, the strength of your EQ is in your hands.

INSTANT TIP

Identify a person who is very different from you (use the Hofstede dimension description if you find them useful). Organise a get-together with them appropriate to your cultures.

Further resources

Chapter 01: What is EI?
The Development Academy EI resources: EI solutions –
articles, assessments, workbooks, coaching and development,
personal development, leadership, business skills and health and
safety applications such as stress management.
http://www.vpde.co.uk

Chapter 02: How does EI affect me as a manager?
Jill Lang: practical applications of individual and team EI
questionnaires as development tools.
jl@infinitycoaches.co.uk; **www.infinitycoaches.co.uk**

Chapter 03: How do I get some EI?
Sandie Pinches: EI in coach/client relationships and in coaching
supervision.
sandie@aboveandbeyondcoaching.com;
http://www.aboveandbeyondcoaching.com

Chapter 04: How do I apply EI?
Dr Edel Ennis: contrasting and comparison of different EI
models, assessments and applications.
e.ennis@ulster.ac.uk; **http://www2.ulster.ac.uk/staff/e.ennis.html**

Chapter 05: What benefits do staff get from developing EI?
Barbara Paterson: contrasting and comparison of the validity

and verification of different EI models and traditional assessments and applications in business. **bepaterson@btinternet.com**

Chapter 06: What benefits do my customers get?
Dr Cathie Palmer-Woodward: EI as a factor in the success of Customer Relationship Marketing; EI at all levels of leadership with regard to talent development and succession planning **cwarturocons@aol.com**

Chapter 07: How does EI accelerate management of change?
Dr Ros McCarthy and Derek Dann: EI as a factor in the success of Change Management interventions
RosMcCCA@aol.com; derekdann@consultationltd.com; http://www.consultationltd.com

Chapter 08: How does EI restore a work/life balance?
http://www.hse.gov.uk/stress/standards/pdfs/leaflet.pdf – Guidelines for employees
http://www.hse.gov.uk/stress/standards/pdfs/standards.pdf – Management guidelines
http://www.hse.gov.uk/gse/sickness.pdf – Learning to be moredynamic under pressure, regulating mood and energy (see **http://www.hunterkane.com/hr_consulting/personal _development/index.htm)**

Chapter 09: How does EI help conflict resolution?
To understand potential root causes of conflict explore the work of Eric Berne, the Founder of Transactional Analysis
http://www.theberne.com/

Chapter 10: How does EI fit with diversity?
If you are in the position of increasing organisational EQ with multi-national and multi-cultural change issues, consider the work of Fons Trompenaars.
http://www.thtconsulting.com/welcome/index.htm

Index